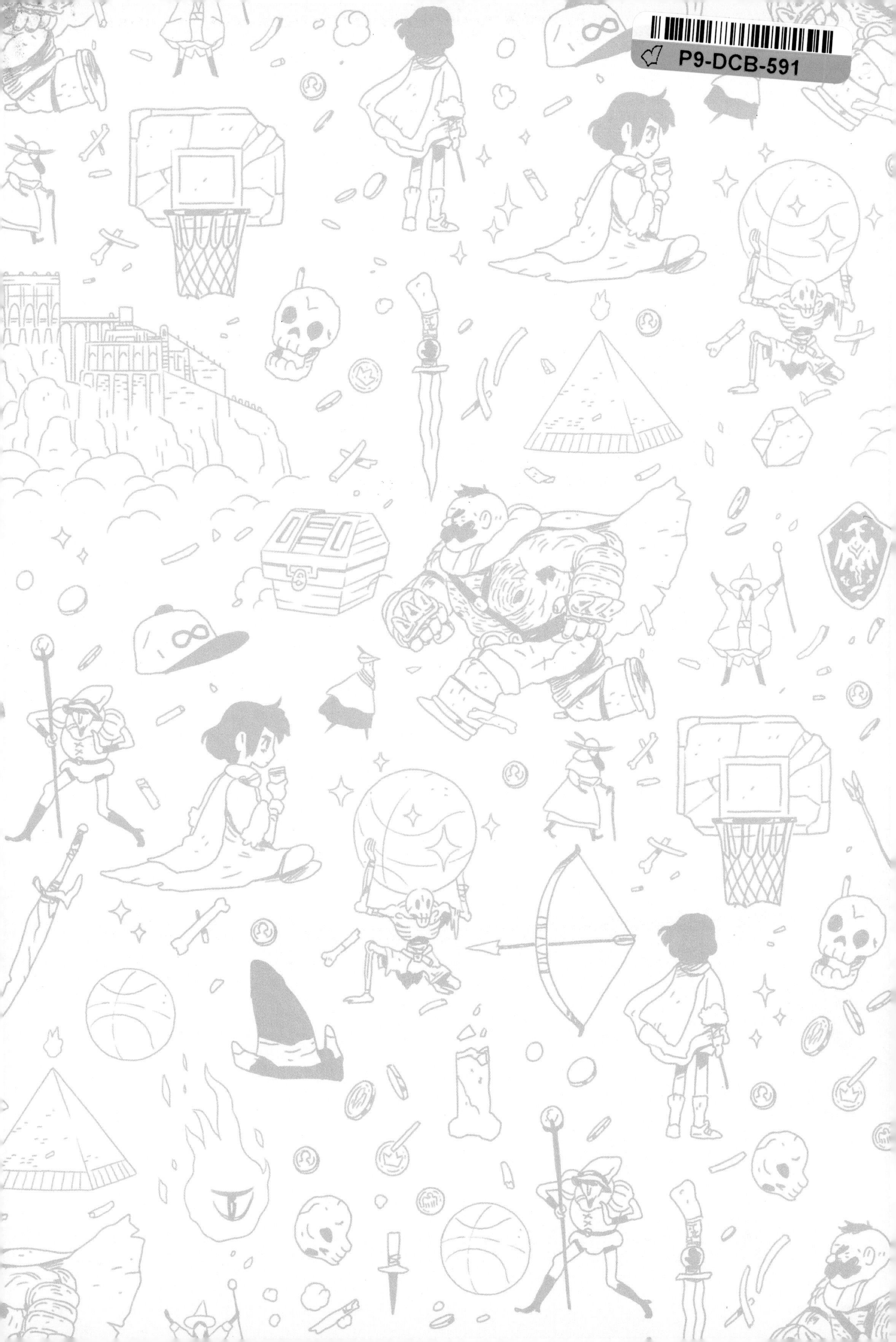

FSC
www.fsc.org

MIX
Paper from
responsible sources
FSC® C101807

FANTASY SPORTS N°1 IS © NOBROW 2015.

THIS IS A FIRST EDITION PUBLISHED IN 2015 BY
NOBROW LTD. 62 GREAT EASTERN STREET, LONDON, EC2A 3QR.

TEXT, CHARACTERS AND ILLUSTRATIONS © SAM BOSMA 2015.
SAM BOSMA HAS ASSERTED HIS RIGHT UNDER THE COPYRIGHT,
DESIGNS AND PATENTS ACT, 1988, TO BE IDENTIFIED AS THE AUTHOR OF THIS WORK.

PUBLISHED IN THE US BY NOBROW (US) INC.

PRINTED IN BELGIUM ON FSC ASSURED PAPER.
ISBN: 978-1-907704-80-2

ORDER FROM WWW.NOBROW.NET

FANTASY SPORTS

NO. 1

SAM BOSMA

NOBROW

LONDON – NEW YORK

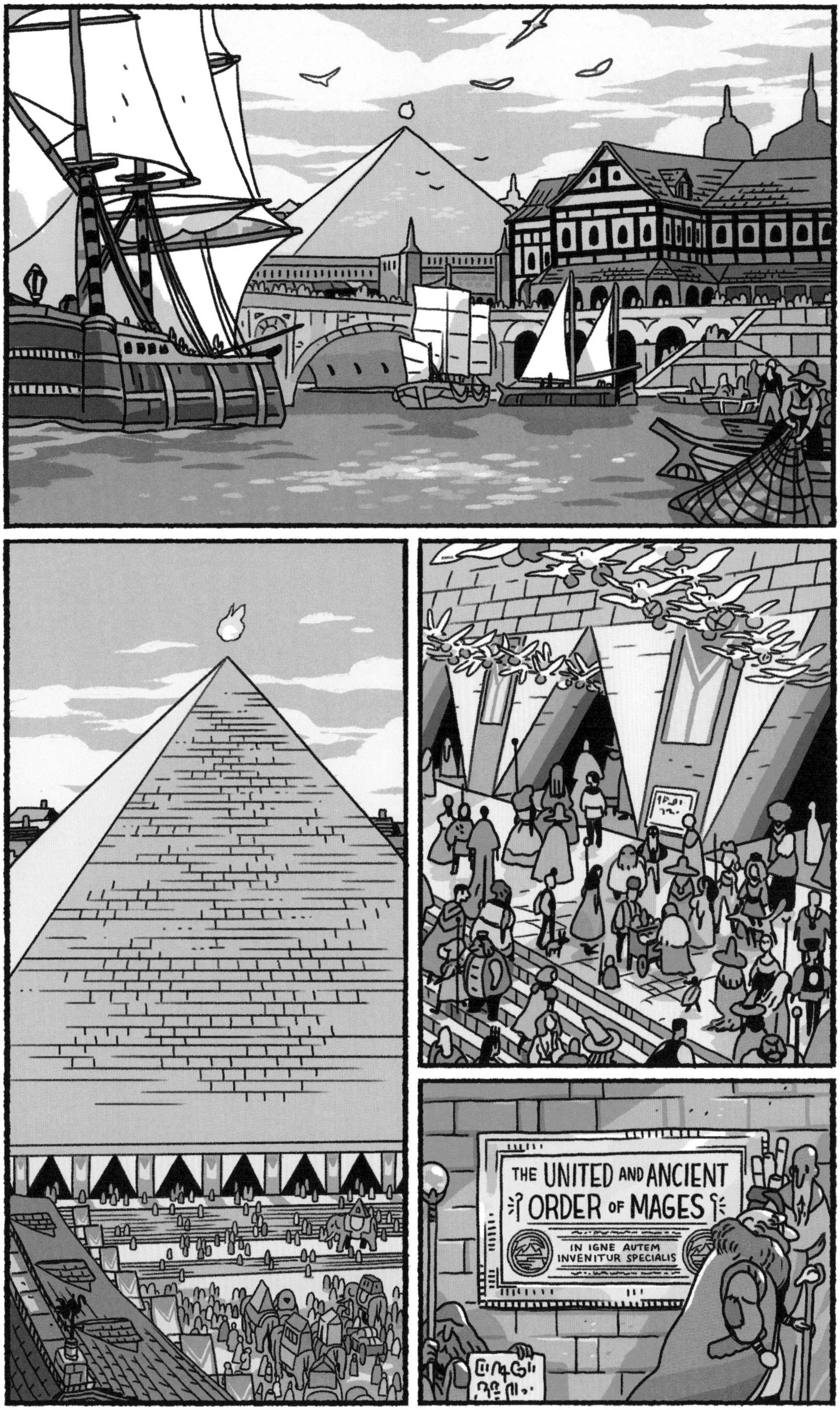
THE UNITED AND ANCIENT
ORDER of MAGES
IN IGNE AUTEM
INVENITUR SPECIALIS

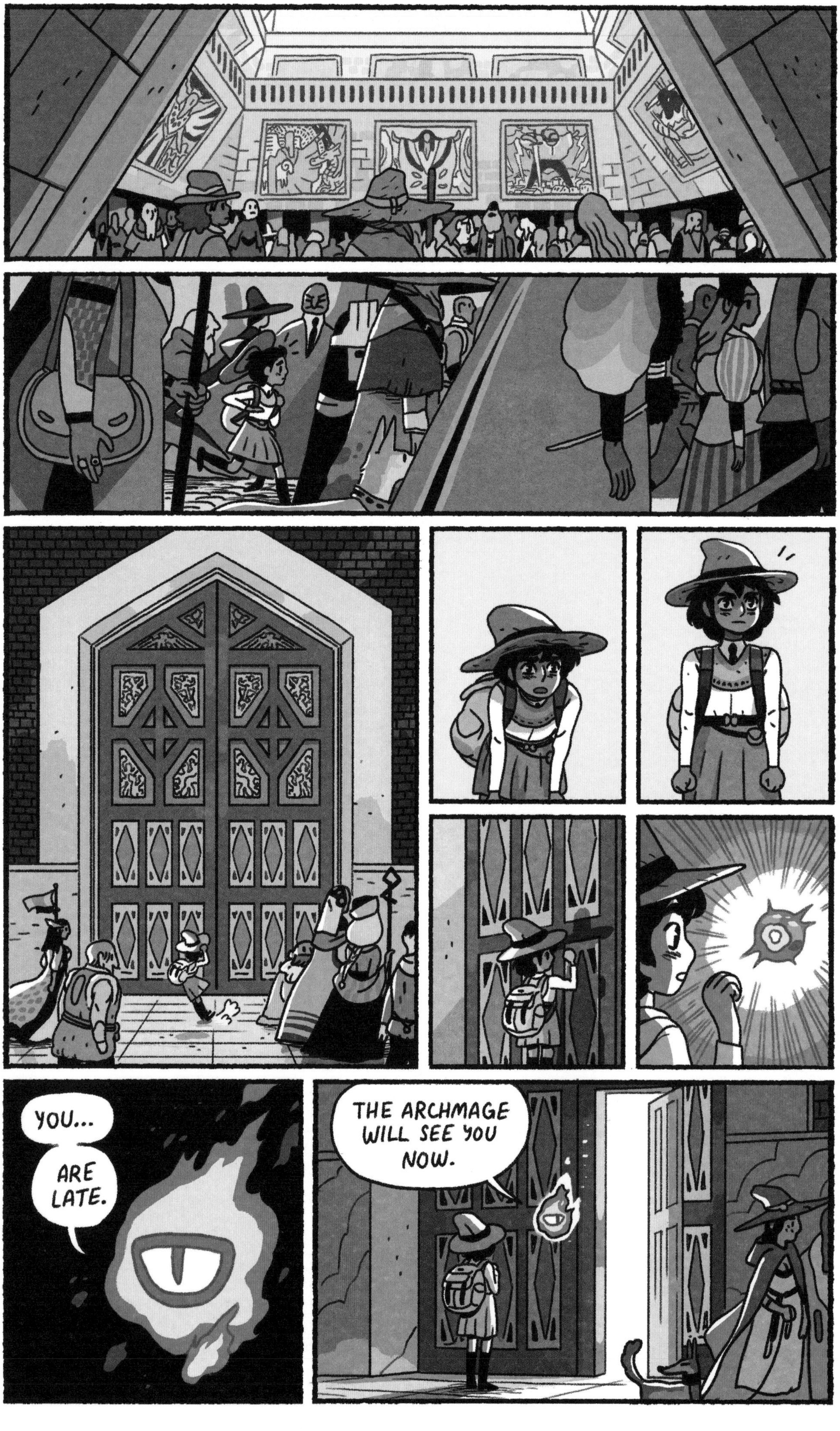
YOU...
ARE LATE.
THE ARCHMAGE WILL SEE YOU NOW.

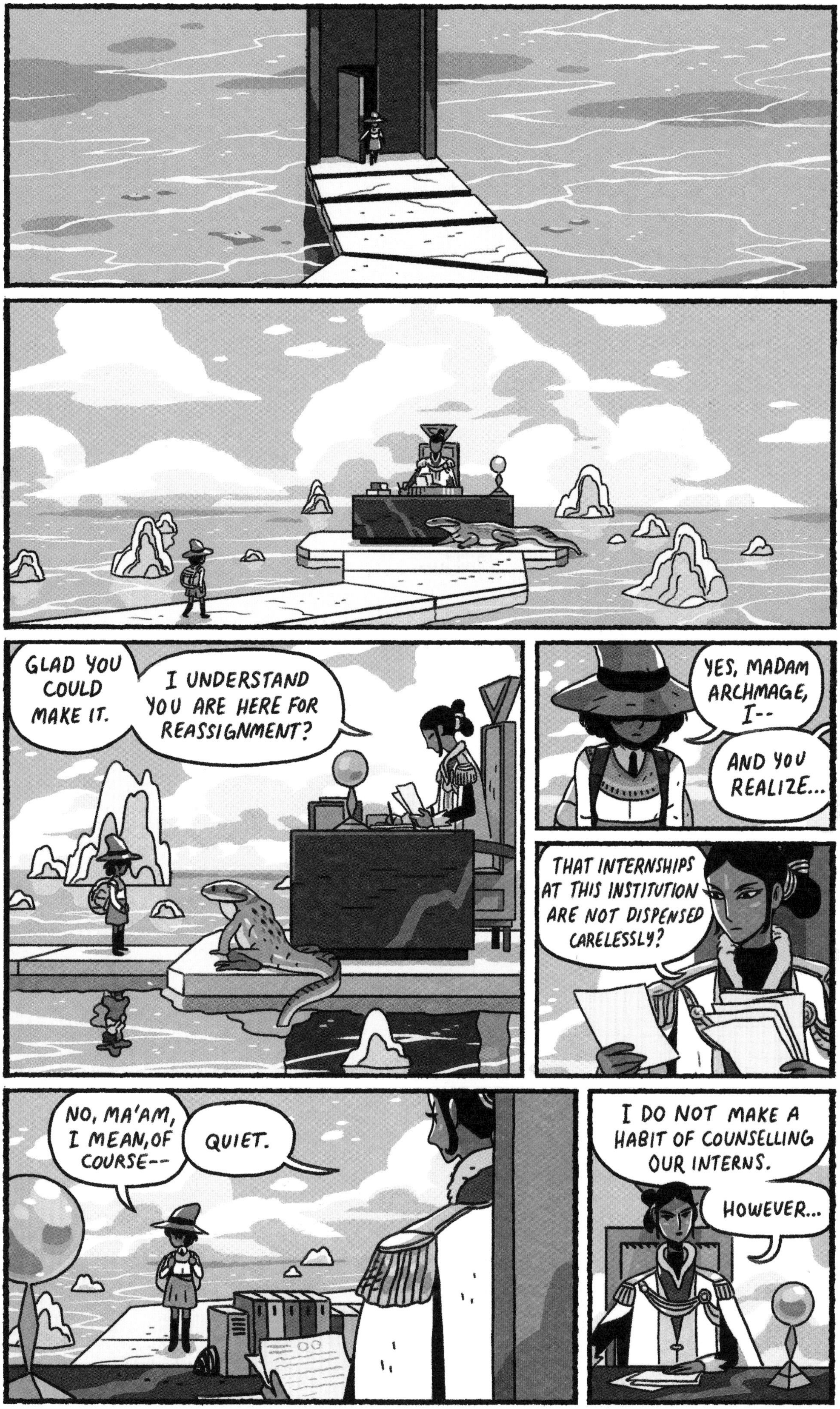
GLAD YOU COULD MAKE IT.
I UNDERSTAND YOU ARE HERE FOR REASSIGNMENT?
YES, MADAM ARCHMAGE, I--
AND YOU REALIZE...
THAT INTERNSHIPS AT THIS INSTITUTION ARE NOT DISPENSED CARELESSLY?
NO, MA'AM, I MEAN, OF COURSE--
QUIET.
I DO NOT MAKE A HABIT OF COUNSELLING OUR INTERNS.
HOWEVER...

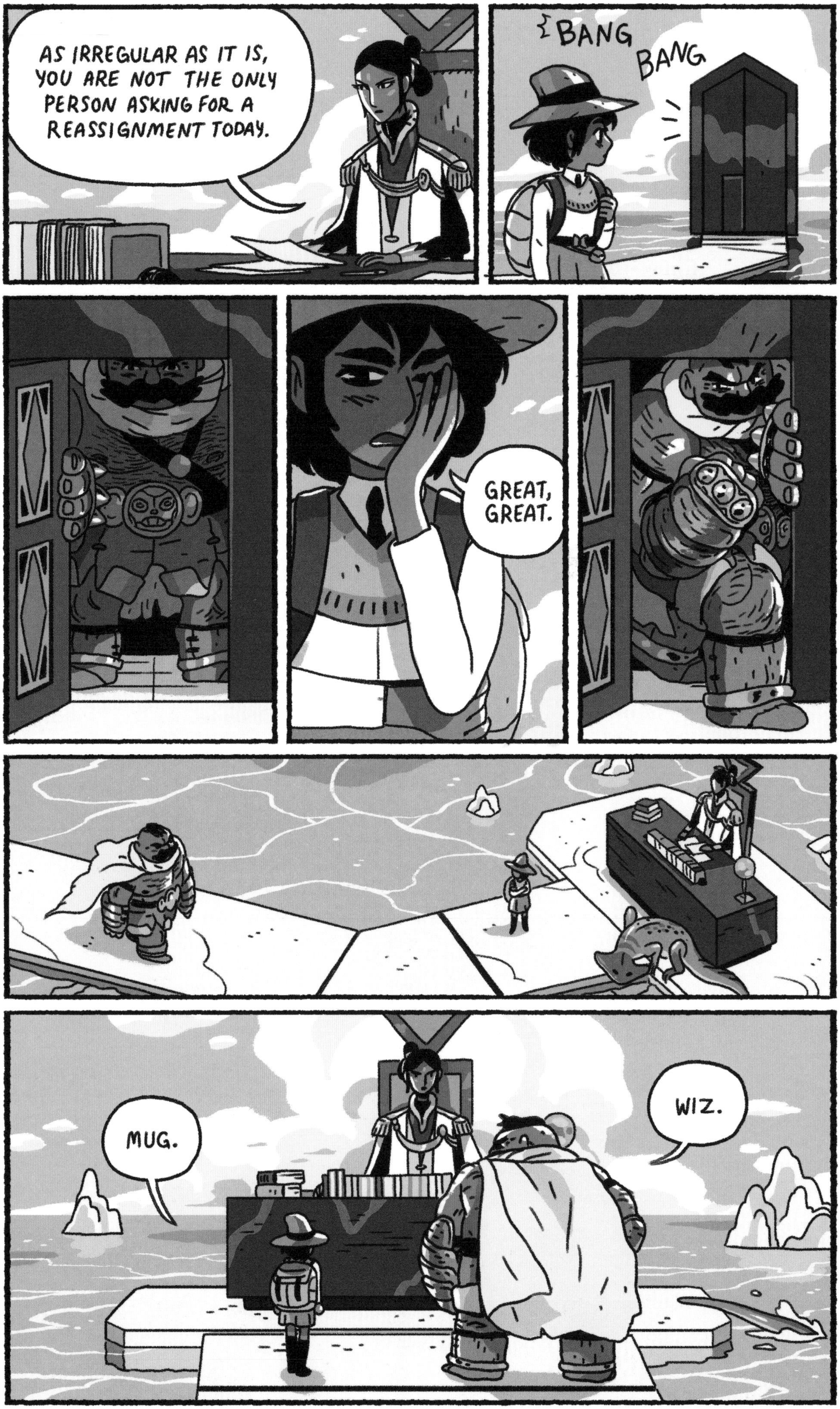
AS IRREGULAR AS IT IS, YOU ARE NOT THE ONLY PERSON ASKING FOR A REASSIGNMENT TODAY.
BANG
BANG
GREAT, GREAT.
MUG.
WIZ.

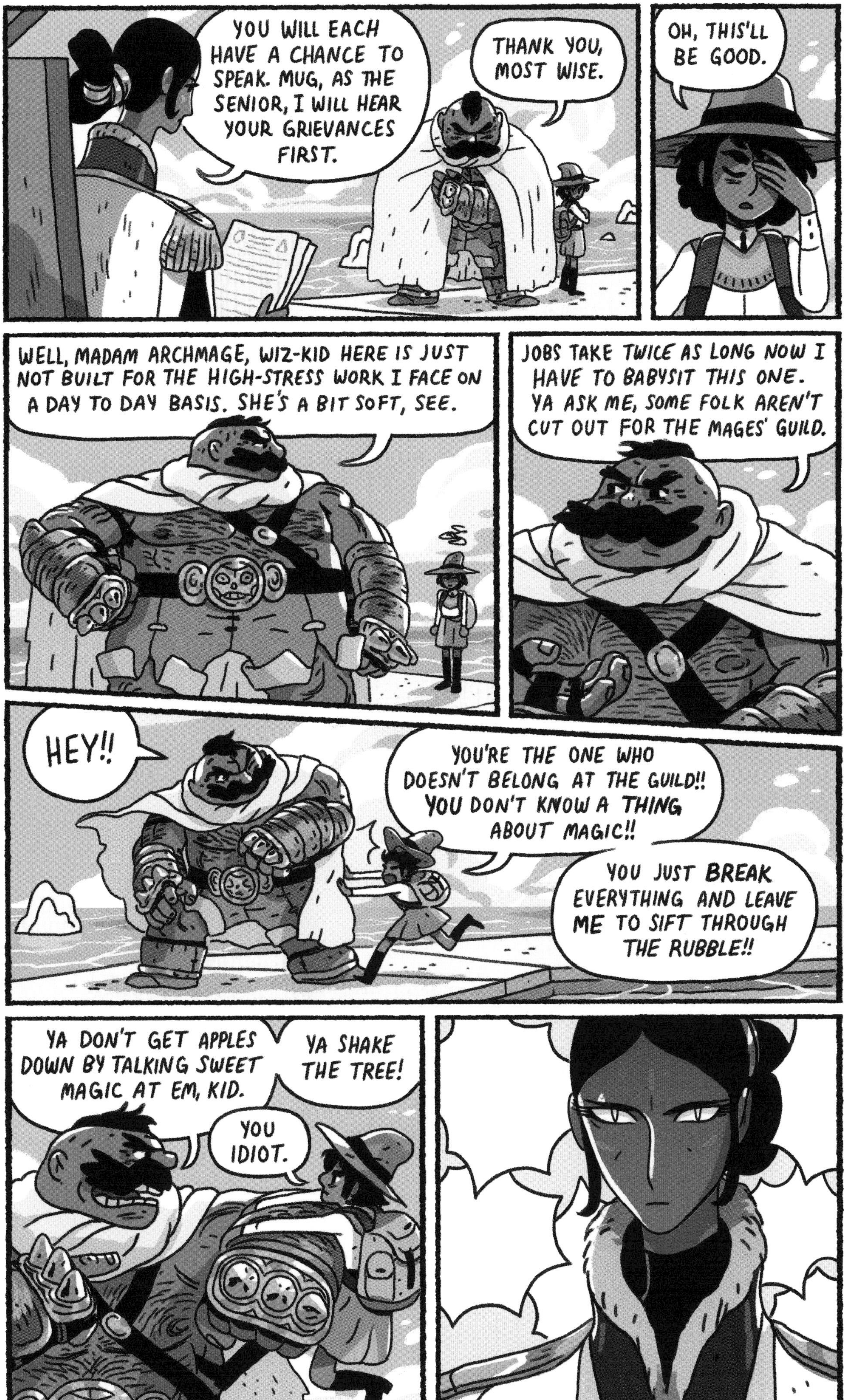
YOU WILL EACH HAVE A CHANCE TO SPEAK. MUG, AS THE SENIOR, I WILL HEAR YOUR GRIEVANCES FIRST.
THANK YOU, MOST WISE.
OH, THIS'LL BE GOOD.
WELL, MADAM ARCHMAGE, WIZ-KID HERE IS JUST NOT BUILT FOR THE HIGH-STRESS WORK I FACE ON A DAY TO DAY BASIS. SHE'S A BIT SOFT, SEE.
JOBS TAKE TWICE AS LONG NOW I HAVE TO BABYSIT THIS ONE. YA ASK ME, SOME FOLK AREN'T CUT OUT FOR THE MAGES' GUILD.
HEY!!
YOU'RE THE ONE WHO DOESN'T BELONG AT THE GUILD!! YOU DON'T KNOW A THING ABOUT MAGIC!!
YOU JUST BREAK EVERYTHING AND LEAVE ME TO SIFT THROUGH THE RUBBLE!!
YA DON'T GET APPLES DOWN BY TALKING SWEET MAGIC AT EM, KID.
YA SHAKE THE TREE!
YOU IDIOT.

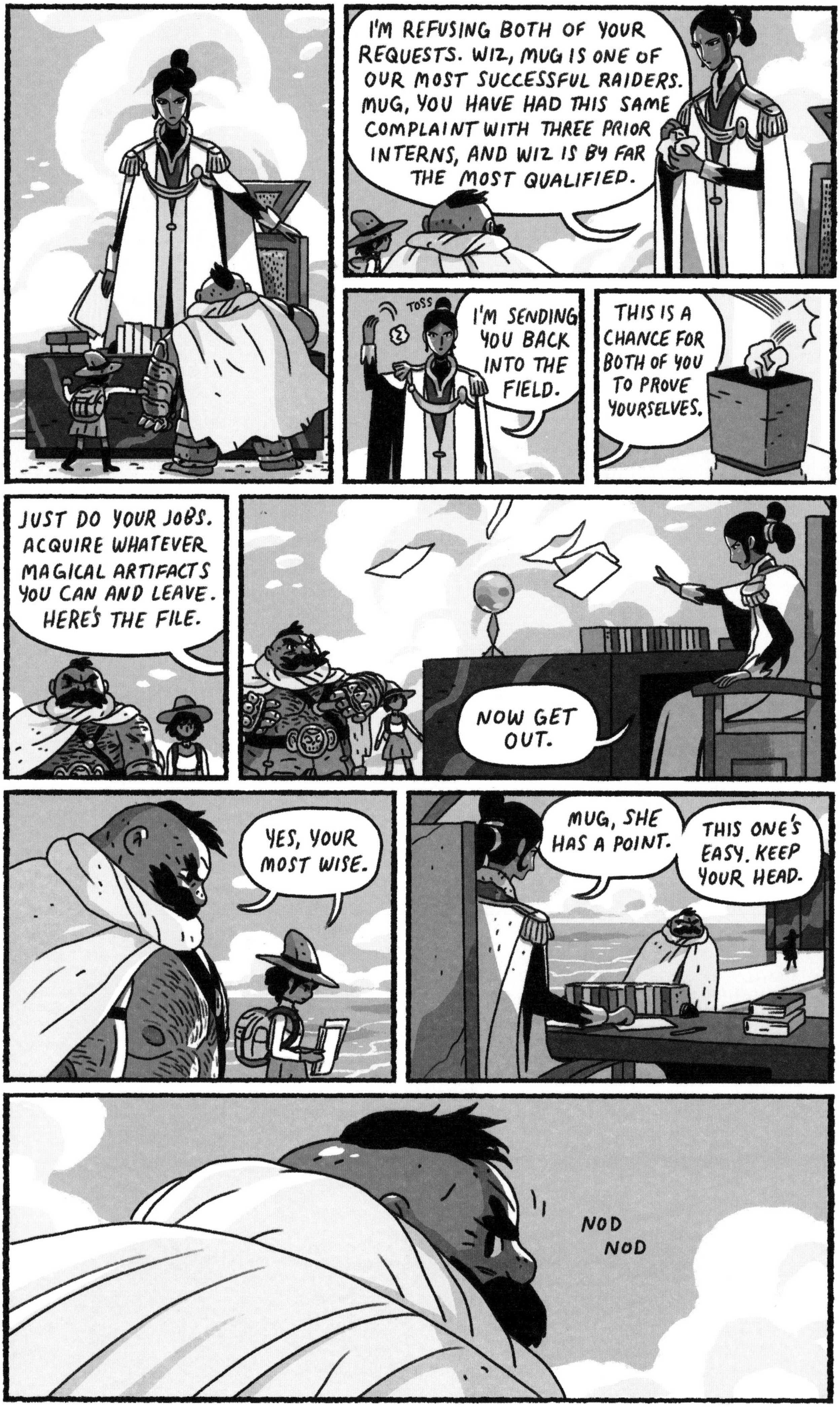
I'M REFUSING BOTH OF YOUR REQUESTS. WIZ, MUG IS ONE OF OUR MOST SUCCESSFUL RAIDERS. MUG, YOU HAVE HAD THIS SAME COMPLAINT WITH THREE PRIOR INTERNS, AND WIZ IS BY FAR THE MOST QUALIFIED.
TOSS
I'M SENDING YOU BACK INTO THE FIELD.
THIS IS A CHANCE FOR BOTH OF YOU TO PROVE YOURSELVES.
JUST DO YOUR JOBS. ACQUIRE WHATEVER MAGICAL ARTIFACTS YOU CAN AND LEAVE. HERE'S THE FILE.
NOW GET OUT.
YES, YOUR MOST WISE.
MUG, SHE HAS A POINT.
THIS ONE'S EASY. KEEP YOUR HEAD.
NOD NOD

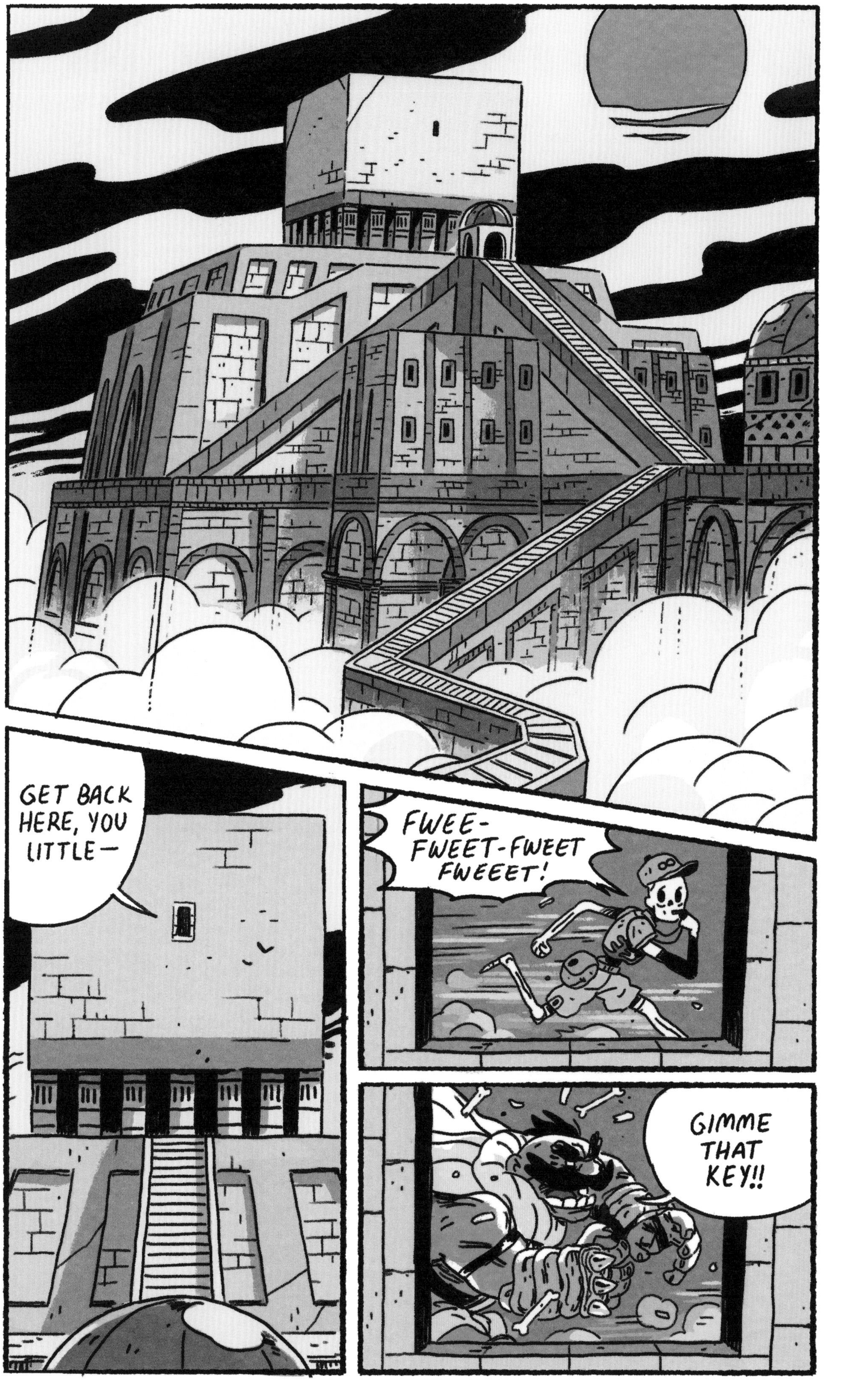
GET BACK HERE, YOU LITTLE—
FWEE- FWEET-FWEET FWEEET!
GIMME THAT KEY!!

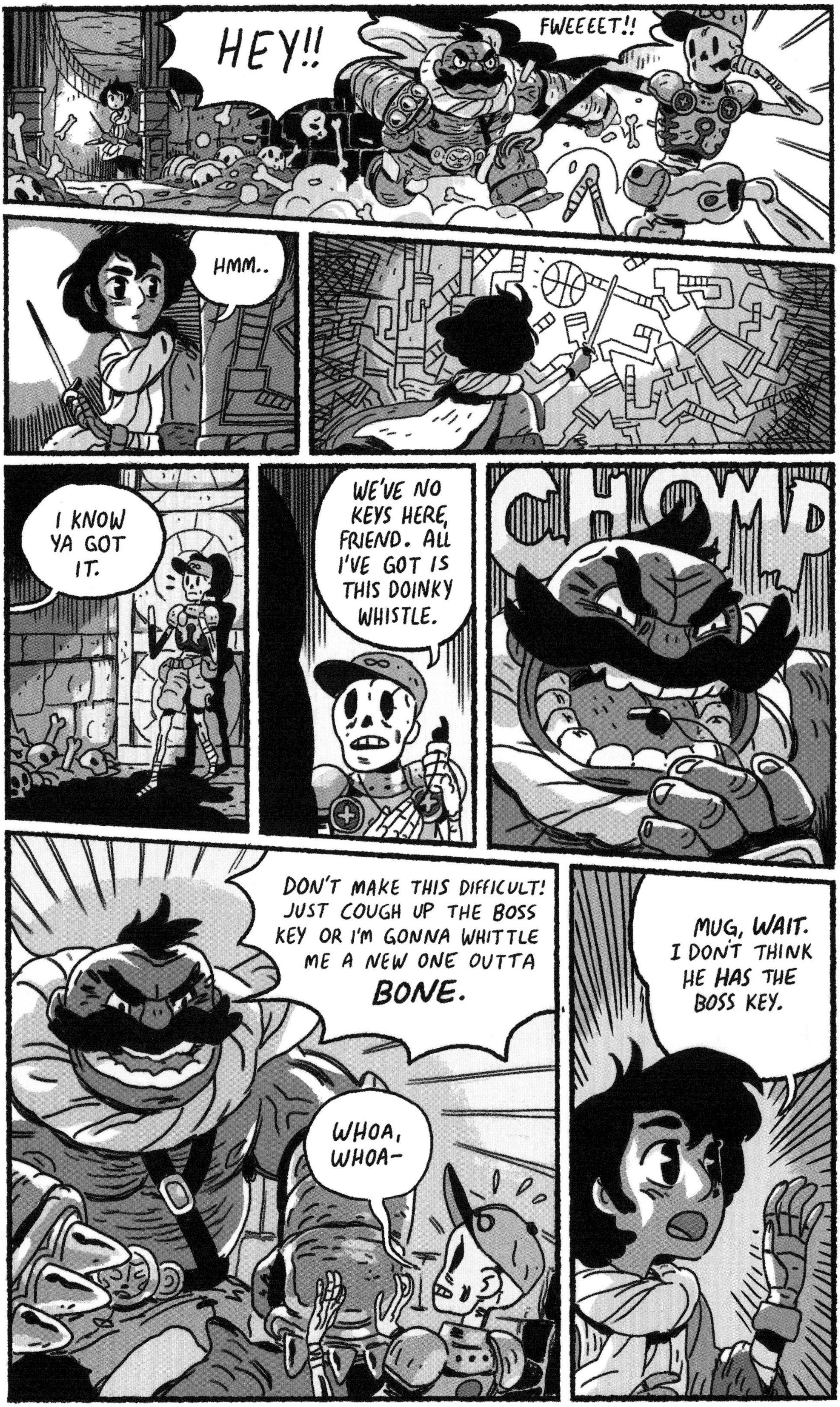
HEY!!
FWEEEET!!
HMM..
I KNOW YA GOT IT.
WE'VE NO KEYS HERE, FRIEND. ALL I'VE GOT IS THIS DOINKY WHISTLE.
CHOMP
DON'T MAKE THIS DIFFICULT! JUST COUGH UP THE BOSS KEY OR I'M GONNA WHITTLE ME A NEW ONE OUTTA BONE.
WHOA, WHOA-
MUG, WAIT. I DON'T THINK HE HAS THE BOSS KEY.

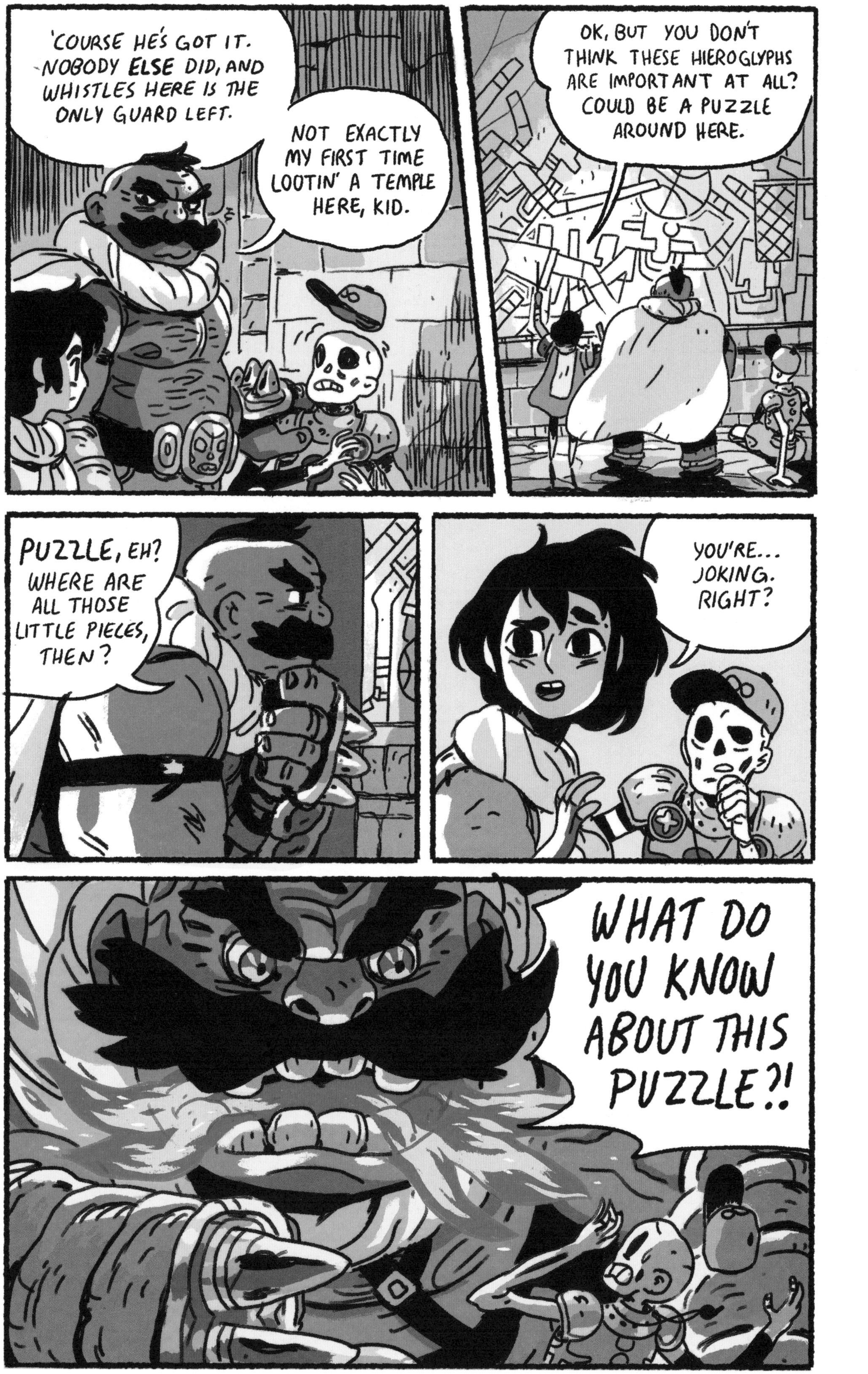
'COURSE HE'S GOT IT. NOBODY ELSE DID, AND WHISTLES HERE IS THE ONLY GUARD LEFT.
NOT EXACTLY MY FIRST TIME LOOTIN' A TEMPLE HERE, KID.
OK, BUT YOU DON'T THINK THESE HIEROGLYPHS ARE IMPORTANT AT ALL? COULD BE A PUZZLE AROUND HERE.
PUZZLE, EH? WHERE ARE ALL THOSE LITTLE PIECES, THEN?
YOU'RE... JOKING. RIGHT?
WHAT DO YOU KNOW ABOUT THIS PUZZLE?!

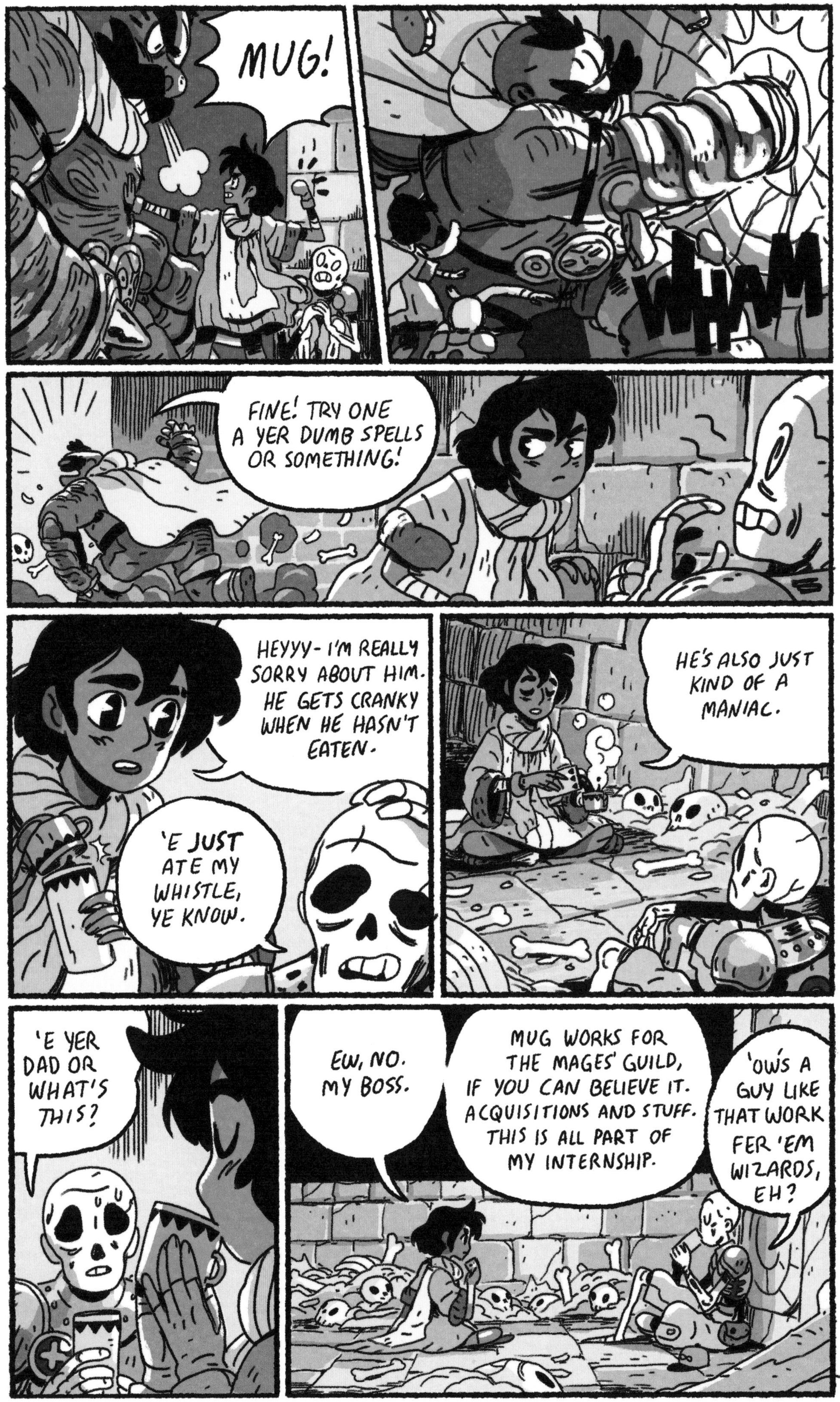
MUG!
WHAM
FINE! TRY ONE A YER DUMB SPELLS OR SOMETHING!
HEYYY- I'M REALLY SORRY ABOUT HIM. HE GETS CRANKY WHEN HE HASN'T EATEN.
'E JUST ATE MY WHISTLE, YE KNOW.
HE'S ALSO JUST KIND OF A MANIAC.
'E YER DAD OR WHAT'S THIS?
EW, NO. MY BOSS.
MUG WORKS FOR THE MAGES' GUILD, IF YOU CAN BELIEVE IT. ACQUISITIONS AND STUFF. THIS IS ALL PART OF MY INTERNSHIP.
'OW'S A GUY LIKE THAT WORK FER 'EM WIZARDS, EH?

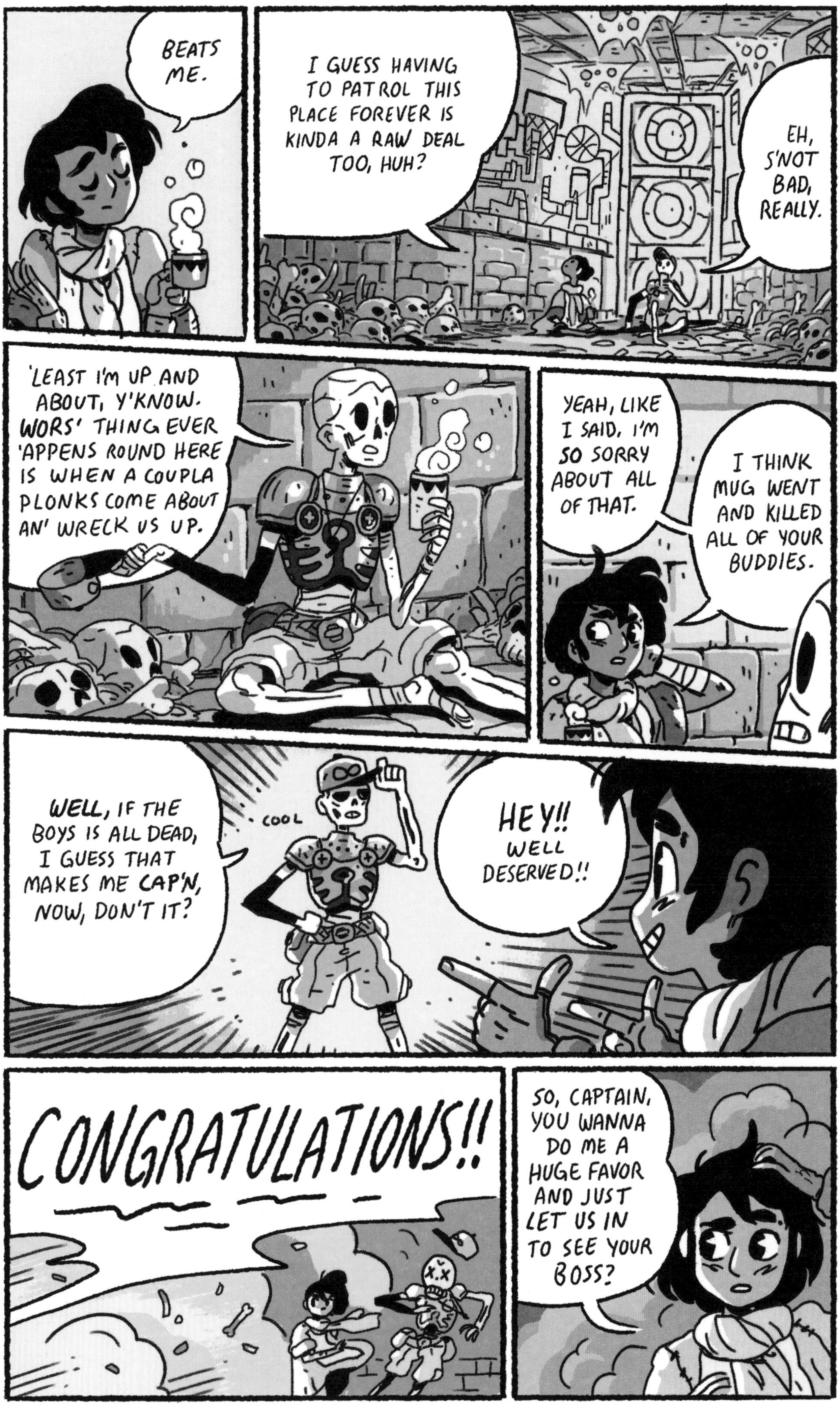
BEATS ME.
I GUESS HAVING TO PATROL THIS PLACE FOREVER IS KINDA A RAW DEAL TOO, HUH?
EH, S'NOT BAD, REALLY.
'LEAST I'M UP AND ABOUT, Y'KNOW. WORS' THING EVER 'APPENS ROUND HERE IS WHEN A COUPLA PLONKS COME ABOUT AN' WRECK US UP.
YEAH, LIKE I SAID, I'M SO SORRY ABOUT ALL OF THAT.
I THINK MUG WENT AND KILLED ALL OF YOUR BUDDIES.
WELL, IF THE BOYS IS ALL DEAD, I GUESS THAT MAKES ME CAP'N, NOW, DON'T IT?
COOL
HEY!! WELL DESERVED!!
CONGRATULATIONS!!
SO, CAPTAIN, YOU WANNA DO ME A HUGE FAVOR AND JUST LET US IN TO SEE YOUR BOSS?

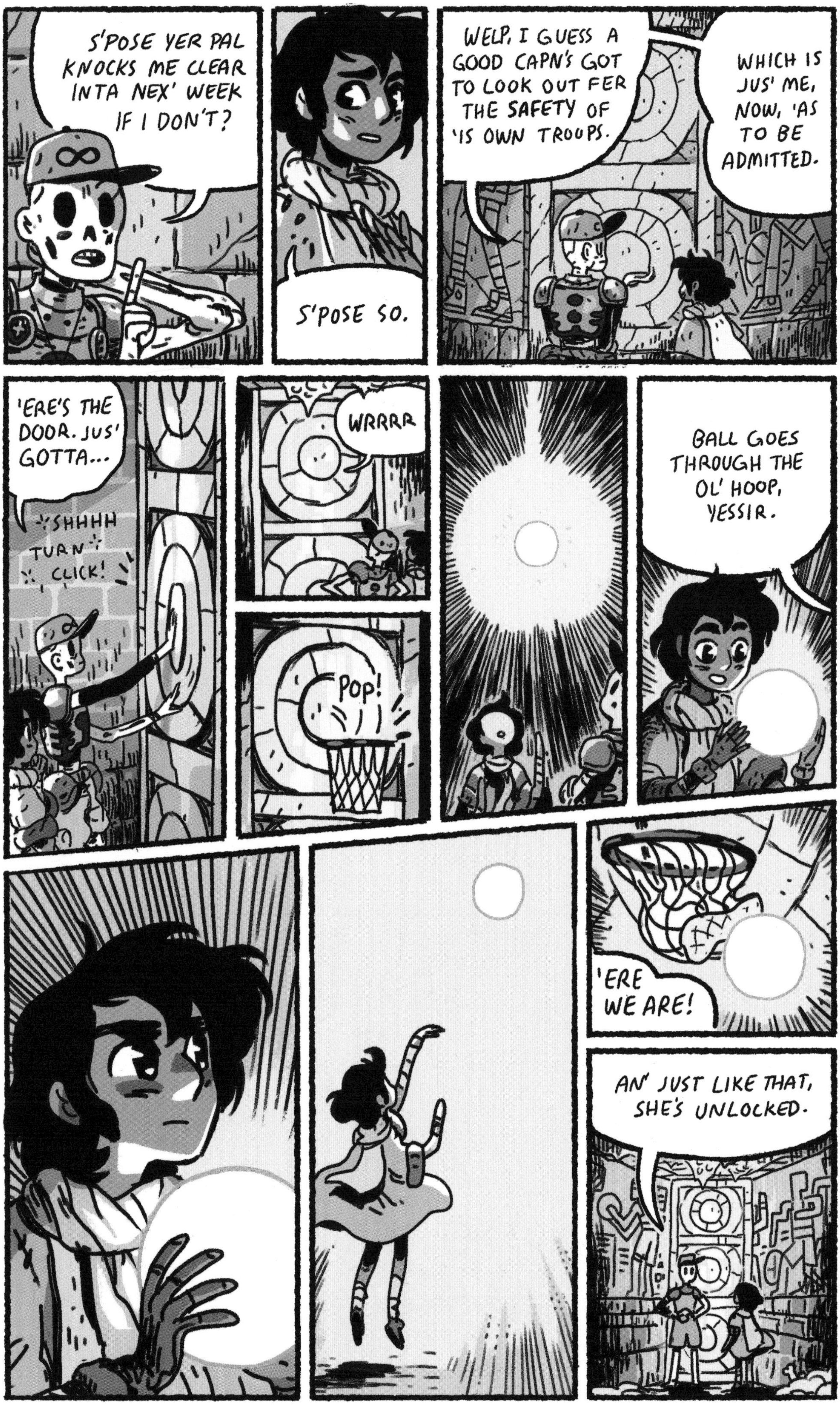
S'POSE YER PAL KNOCKS ME CLEAR INTA NEX' WEEK IF I DON'T?
S'POSE SO.
WELP, I GUESS A GOOD CAPN'S GOT TO LOOK OUT FER THE SAFETY OF 'IS OWN TROUPS.
WHICH IS JUS' ME, NOW, 'AS TO BE ADMITTED.
'ERE'S THE DOOR. JUS' GOTTA...
SHHHH
TURN
CLICK!
WRRRR
POP!
BALL GOES THROUGH THE OL' HOOP, YESSIR.
'ERE WE ARE!
AN' JUST LIKE THAT, SHE'S UNLOCKED.

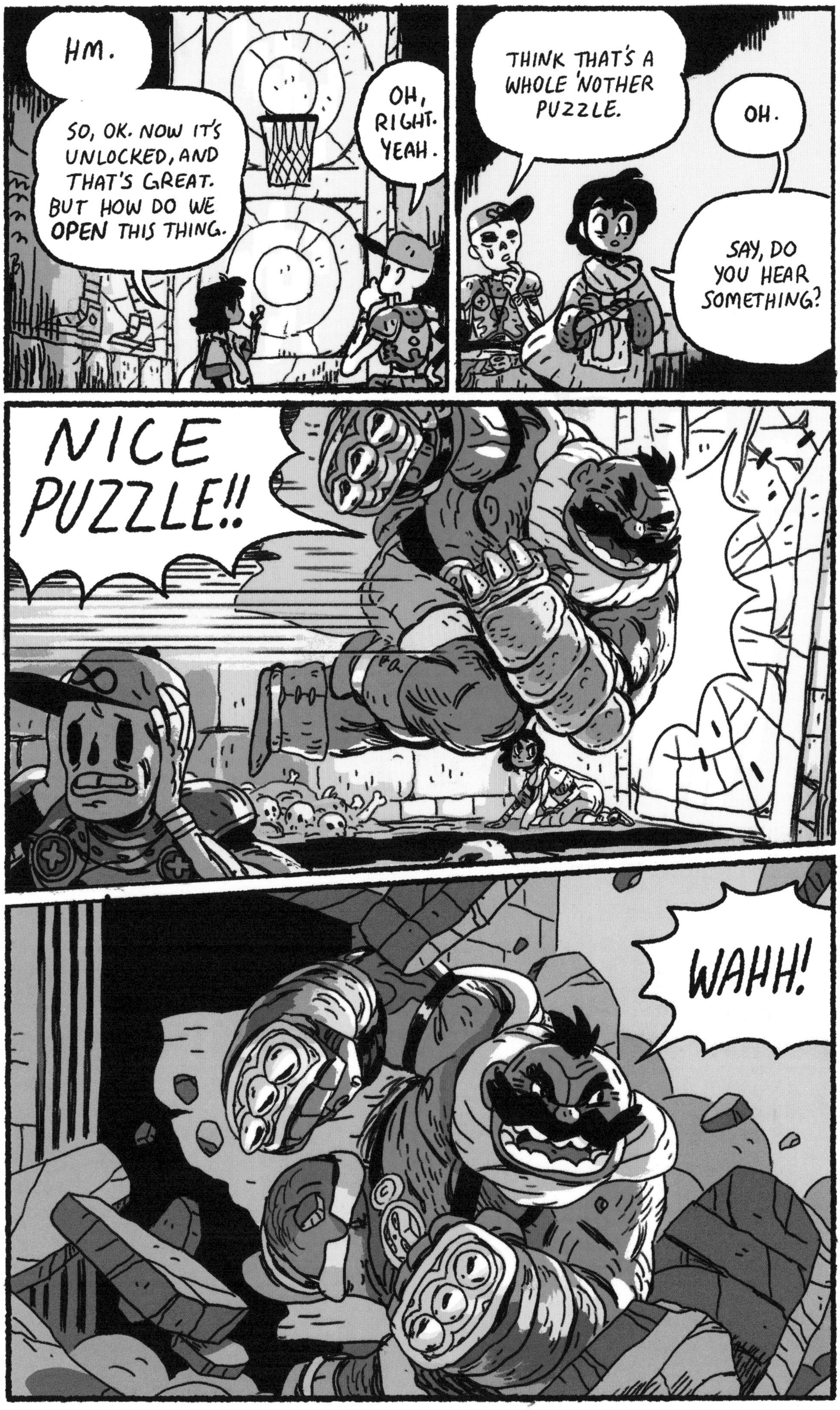
HM.
SO, OK. NOW IT'S UNLOCKED, AND THAT'S GREAT. BUT HOW DO WE OPEN THIS THING.
OH, RIGHT. YEAH.
THINK THAT'S A WHOLE 'NOTHER PUZZLE.
OH.
SAY, DO YOU HEAR SOMETHING?
NICE PUZZLE!!
WAHH!

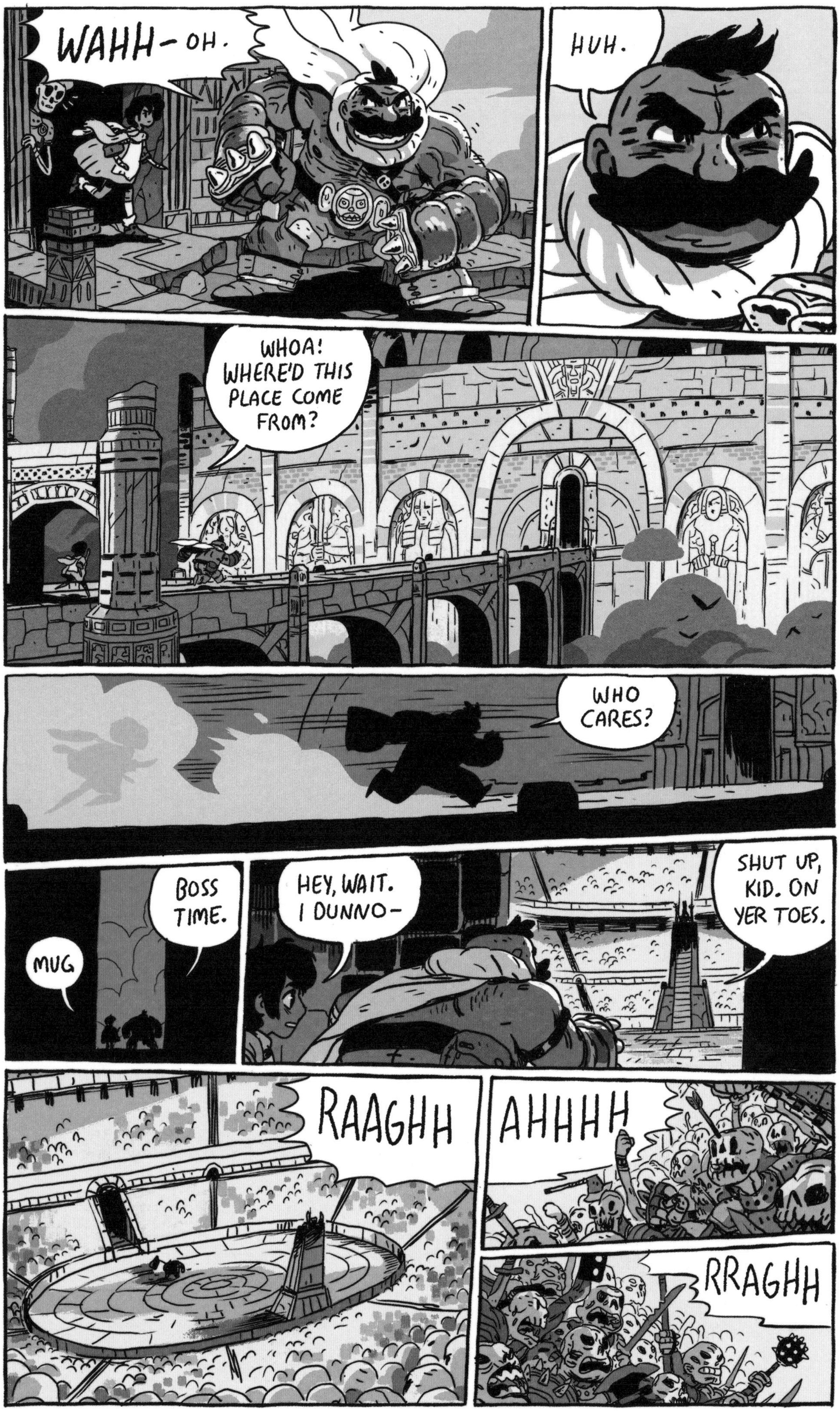
WAHH-OH.
HUH.
WHOA! WHERE'D THIS PLACE COME FROM?
WHO CARES?
MUG
BOSS TIME.
HEY, WAIT. I DUNNO-
SHUT UP, KID. ON YER TOES.
RAAGHH
AHHHH
RRAGHH

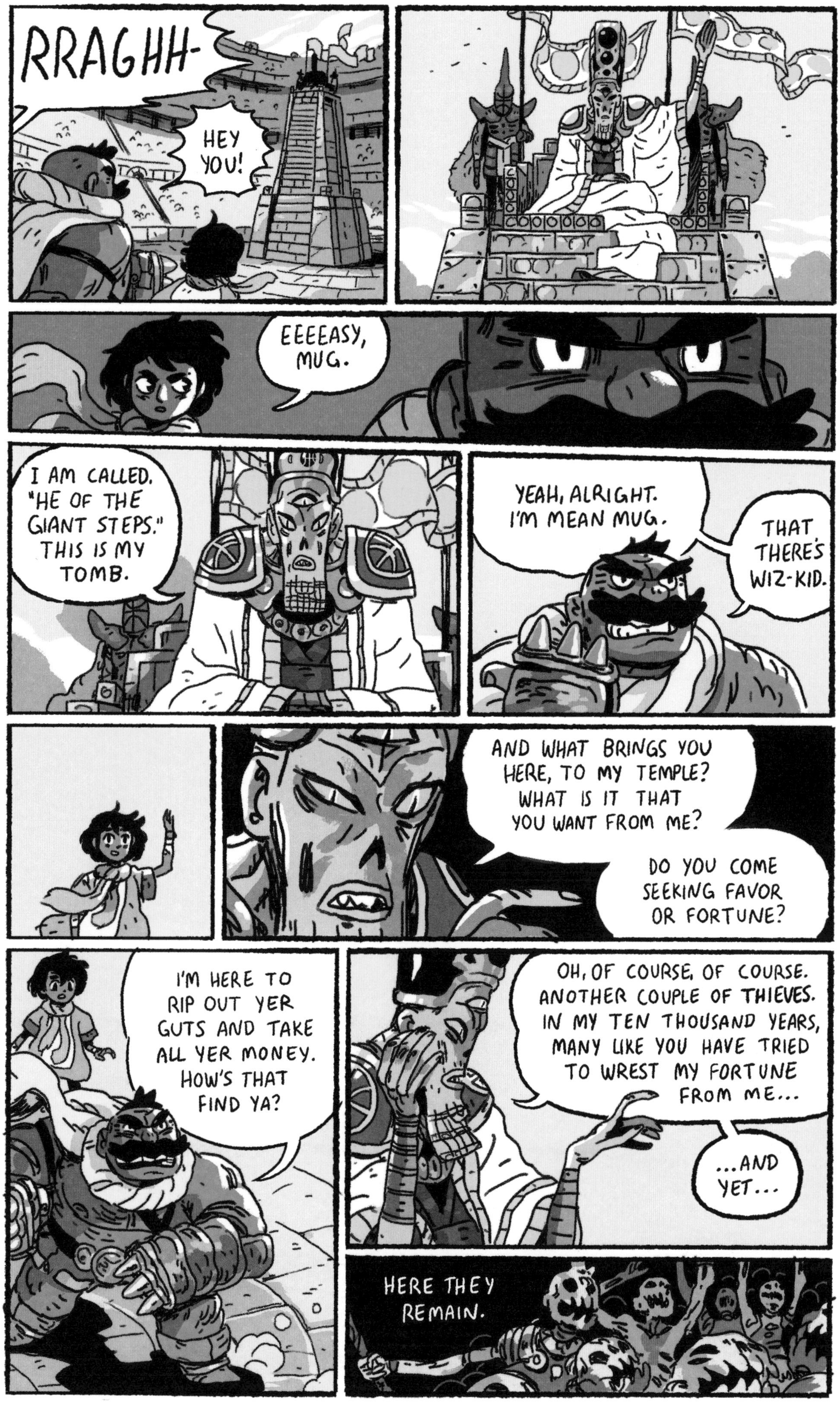
RRAGHH-
HEY YOU!
EEEEASY, MUG.
I AM CALLED. "HE OF THE GIANT STEPS." THIS IS MY TOMB.
YEAH, ALRIGHT. I'M MEAN MUG.
THAT THERE'S WIZ-KID.
AND WHAT BRINGS YOU HERE, TO MY TEMPLE? WHAT IS IT THAT YOU WANT FROM ME?
DO YOU COME SEEKING FAVOR OR FORTUNE?
I'M HERE TO RIP OUT YER GUTS AND TAKE ALL YER MONEY. HOW'S THAT FIND YA?
OH, OF COURSE, OF COURSE. ANOTHER COUPLE OF THIEVES. IN MY TEN THOUSAND YEARS, MANY LIKE YOU HAVE TRIED TO WREST MY FORTUNE FROM ME...
...AND YET...
HERE THEY REMAIN.

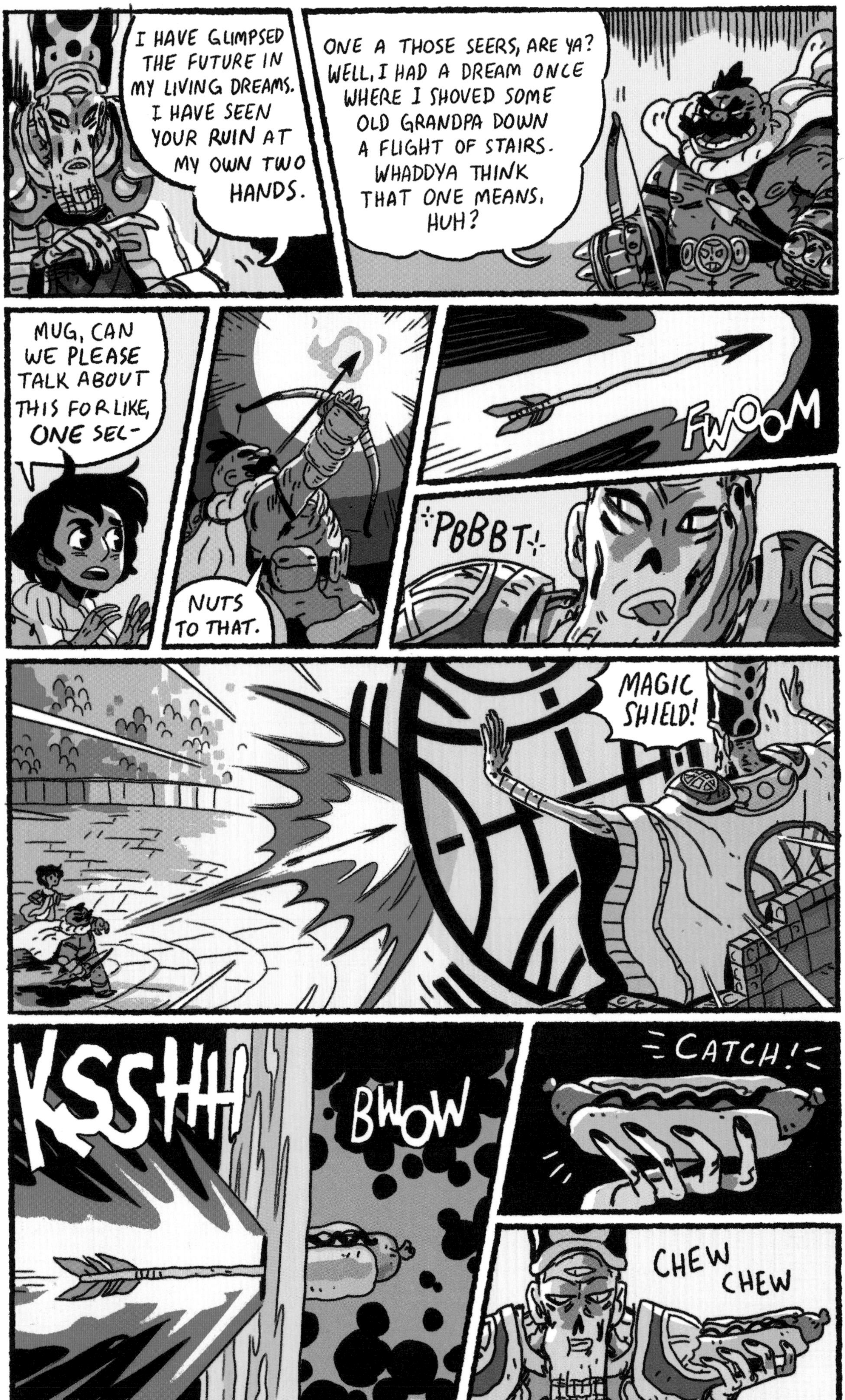
I HAVE GLIMPSED THE FUTURE IN MY LIVING DREAMS. I HAVE SEEN YOUR RUIN AT MY OWN TWO HANDS.
ONE A THOSE SEERS, ARE YA? WELL, I HAD A DREAM ONCE WHERE I SHOVED SOME OLD GRANDPA DOWN A FLIGHT OF STAIRS. WHADDYA THINK THAT ONE MEANS, HUH?
MUG, CAN WE PLEASE TALK ABOUT THIS FOR LIKE, ONE SEC-
NUTS TO THAT.
FWOOM
PBBBT
MAGIC SHIELD!
KSSHH
BWOW
CATCH!
CHEW CHEW

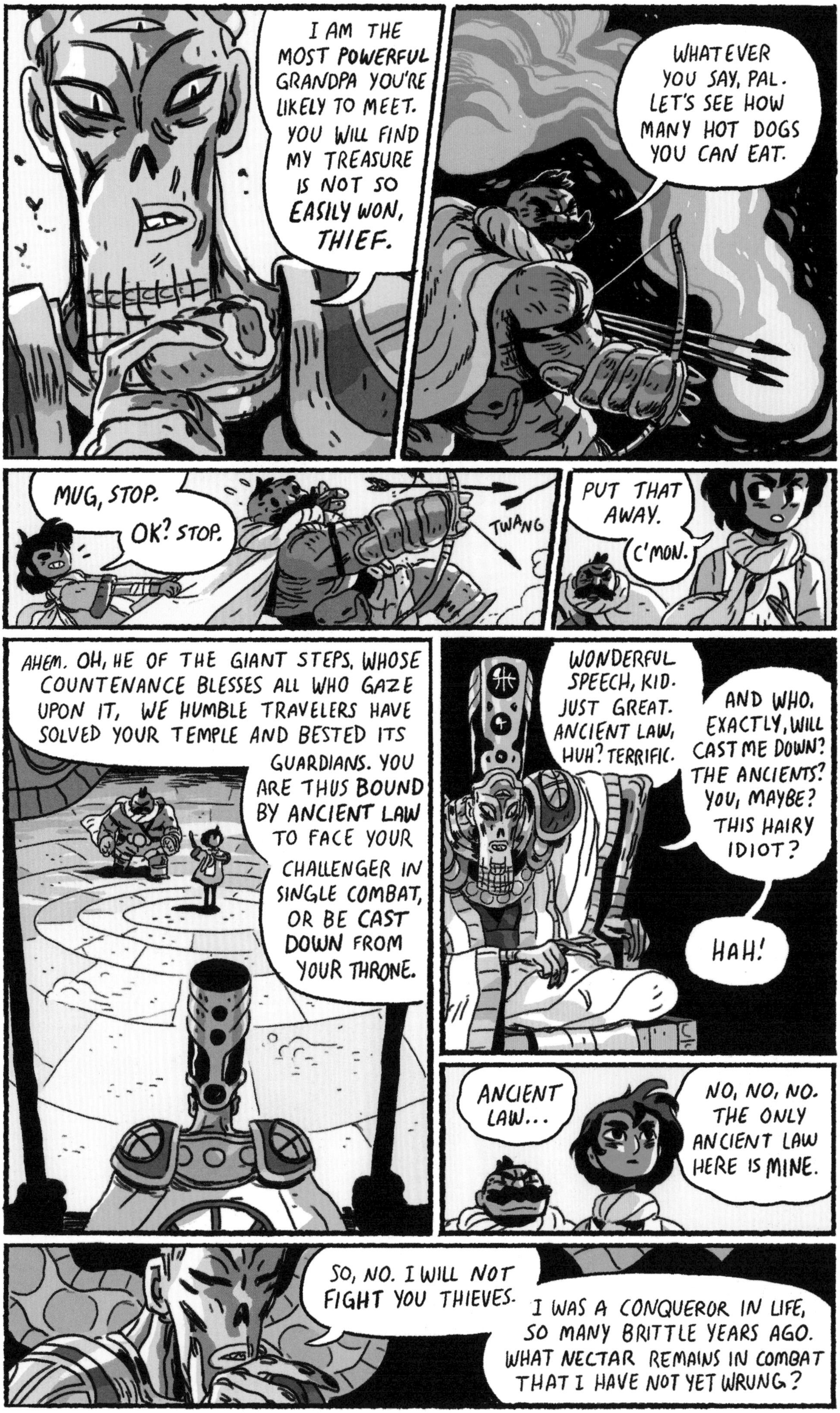
I AM THE MOST POWERFUL GRANDPA YOU'RE LIKELY TO MEET. YOU WILL FIND MY TREASURE IS NOT SO EASILY WON, THIEF.
WHATEVER YOU SAY, PAL. LET'S SEE HOW MANY HOT DOGS YOU CAN EAT.
MUG, STOP.
OK? STOP.
TWANG
PUT THAT AWAY.
C'MON.
AHEM. OH, HE OF THE GIANT STEPS, WHOSE COUNTENANCE BLESSES ALL WHO GAZE UPON IT, WE HUMBLE TRAVELERS HAVE SOLVED YOUR TEMPLE AND BESTED ITS GUARDIANS. YOU ARE THUS BOUND BY ANCIENT LAW TO FACE YOUR CHALLENGER IN SINGLE COMBAT, OR BE CAST DOWN FROM YOUR THRONE.
WONDERFUL SPEECH, KID. JUST GREAT. ANCIENT LAW, HUH? TERRIFIC.
AND WHO, EXACTLY, WILL CAST ME DOWN? THE ANCIENTS? YOU, MAYBE? THIS HAIRY IDIOT?
HAH!
ANCIENT LAW...
NO, NO, NO. THE ONLY ANCIENT LAW HERE IS MINE.
SO, NO. I WILL NOT FIGHT YOU THIEVES.
I WAS A CONQUEROR IN LIFE, SO MANY BRITTLE YEARS AGO. WHAT NECTAR REMAINS IN COMBAT THAT I HAVE NOT YET WRUNG?

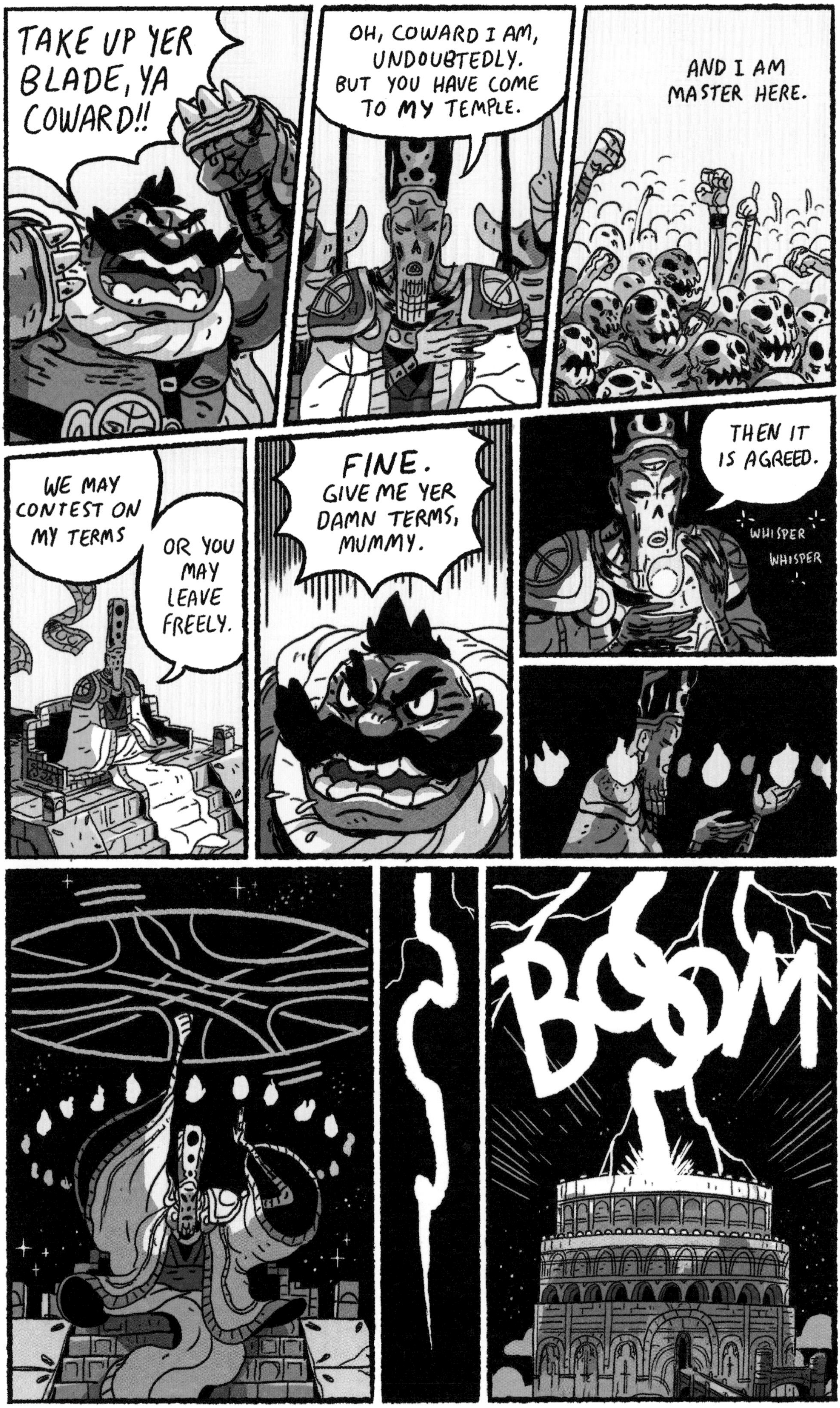
TAKE UP YER BLADE, YA COWARD!!
OH, COWARD I AM, UNDOUBTEDLY. BUT YOU HAVE COME TO MY TEMPLE.
AND I AM MASTER HERE.
WE MAY CONTEST ON MY TERMS
OR YOU MAY LEAVE FREELY.
FINE. GIVE ME YER DAMN TERMS, MUMMY.
THEN IT IS AGREED.
WHISPER
WHISPER
BOOOM

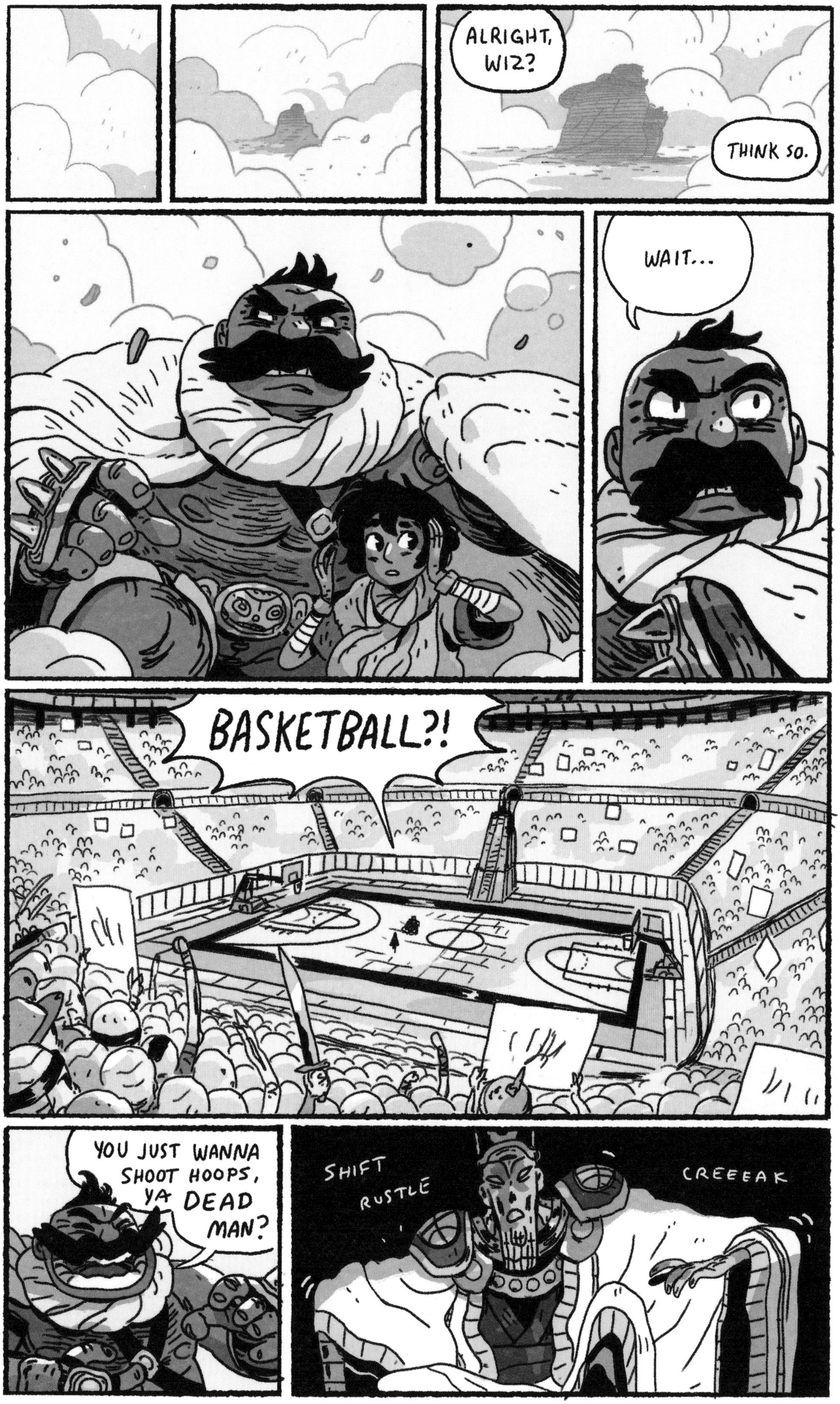
ALRIGHT, WIZ?
THINK SO.
WAIT...
BASKETBALL?!
YOU JUST WANNA SHOOT HOOPS, YA DEAD MAN?
SHIFT
RUSTLE
CREEEAK

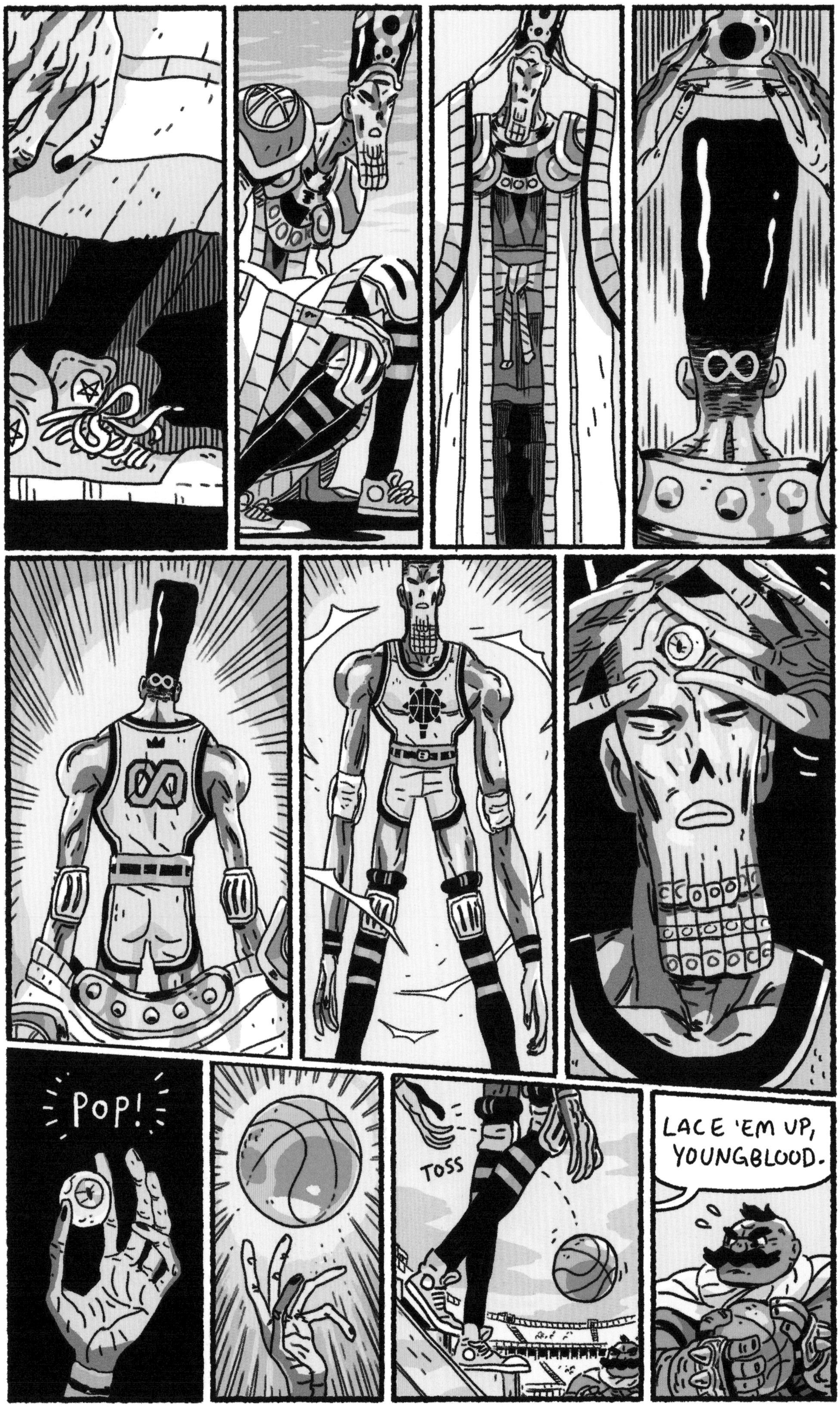
POP!
TOSS
LACE 'EM UP, YOUNGBLOOD.

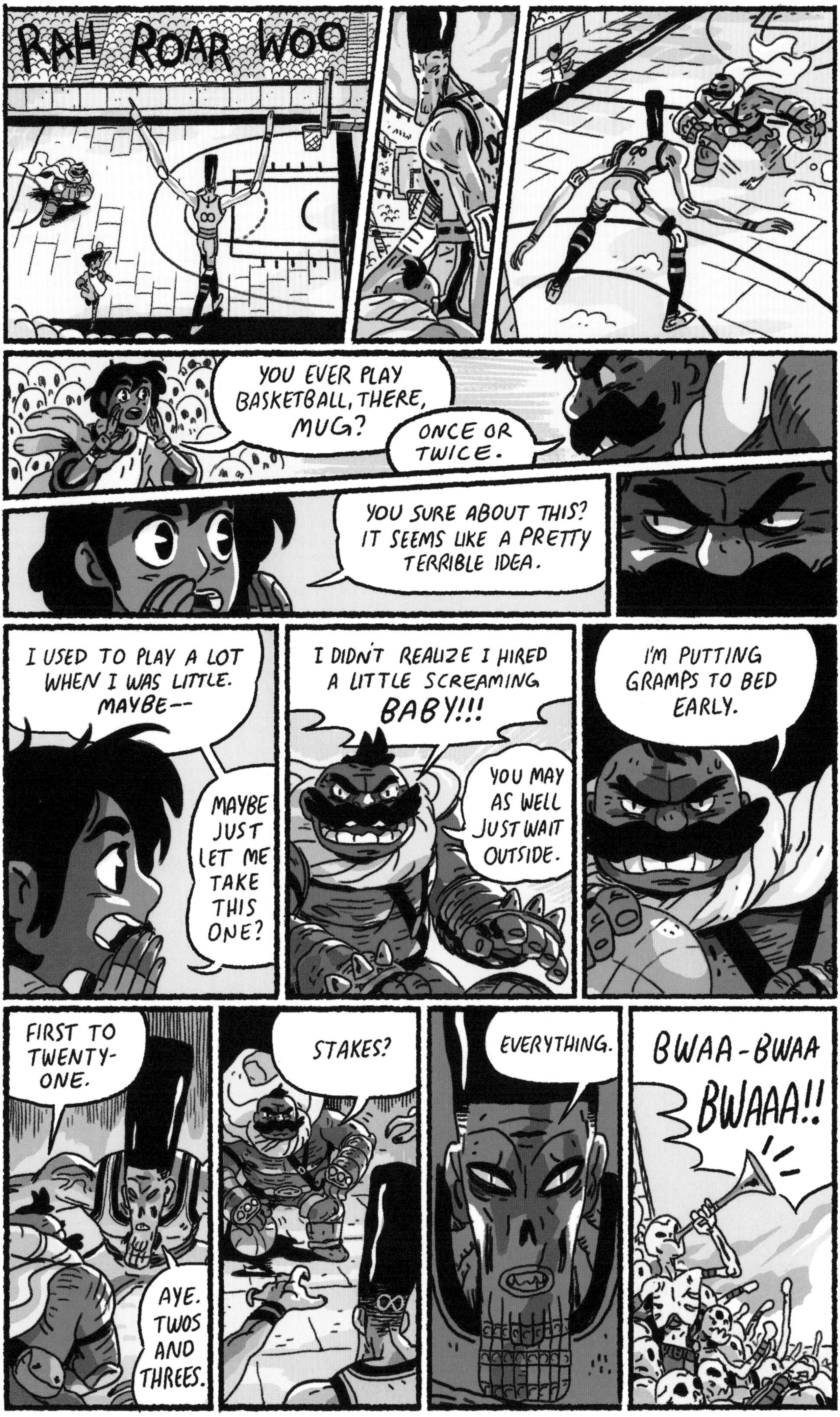
RAH ROAR WOO
YOU EVER PLAY BASKETBALL, THERE, MUG?
ONCE OR TWICE.
YOU SURE ABOUT THIS? IT SEEMS LIKE A PRETTY TERRIBLE IDEA.
I USED TO PLAY A LOT WHEN I WAS LITTLE. MAYBE--
MAYBE JUST LET ME TAKE THIS ONE?
I DIDN'T REALIZE I HIRED A LITTLE SCREAMING BABY!!!
YOU MAY AS WELL JUST WAIT OUTSIDE.
I'M PUTTING GRAMPS TO BED EARLY.
FIRST TO TWENTY-ONE.
AYE. TWOS AND THREES.
STAKES?
EVERYTHING.
BWAA-BWAA BWAAA!!

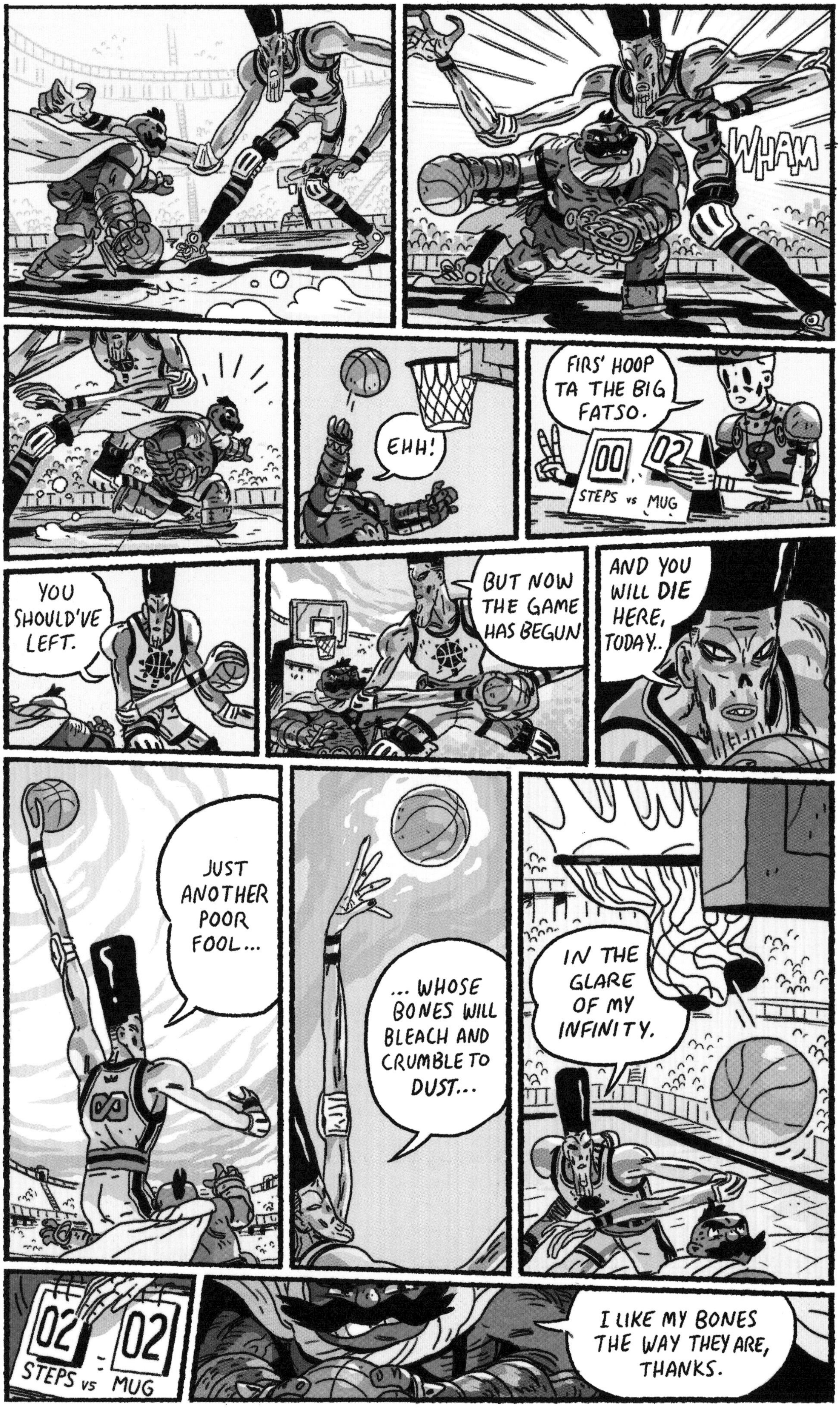
WHAM
FIRS' HOOP TA THE BIG FATSO.
EHH!
00 02
STEPS vs MUG
YOU SHOULD'VE LEFT.
BUT NOW THE GAME HAS BEGUN
AND YOU WILL DIE HERE, TODAY..
JUST ANOTHER POOR FOOL...
... WHOSE BONES WILL BLEACH AND CRUMBLE TO DUST...
IN THE GLARE OF MY INFINITY.
02 02
STEPS vs MUG
I LIKE MY BONES THE WAY THEY ARE, THANKS.

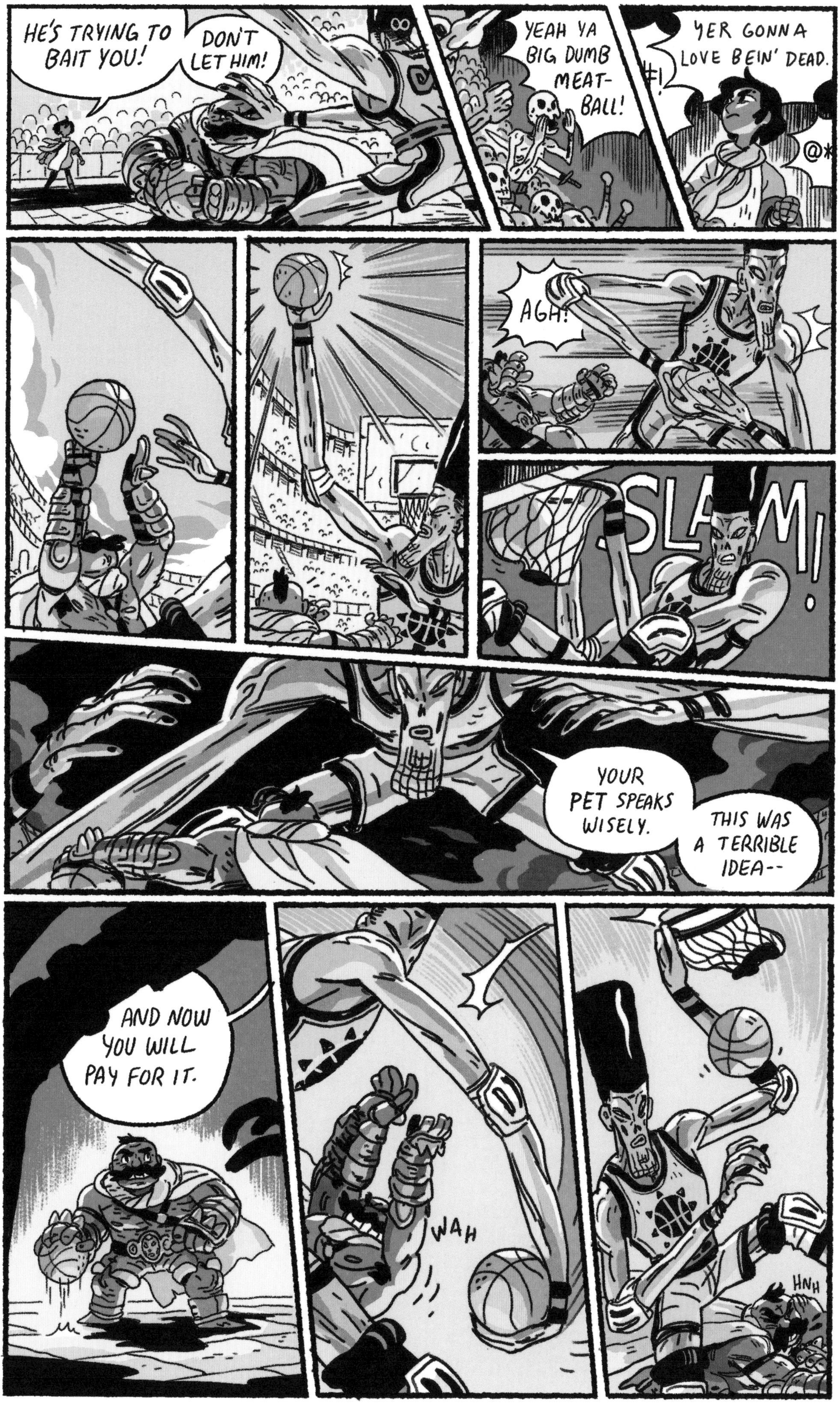
HE'S TRYING TO BAIT YOU!
DON'T LET HIM!
YEAH YA BIG DUMB MEAT-BALL!
YER GONNA LOVE BEIN' DEAD.
AGH!
SLAM!
YOUR PET SPEAKS WISELY.
THIS WAS A TERRIBLE IDEA--
AND NOW YOU WILL PAY FOR IT.
WAH
HNH

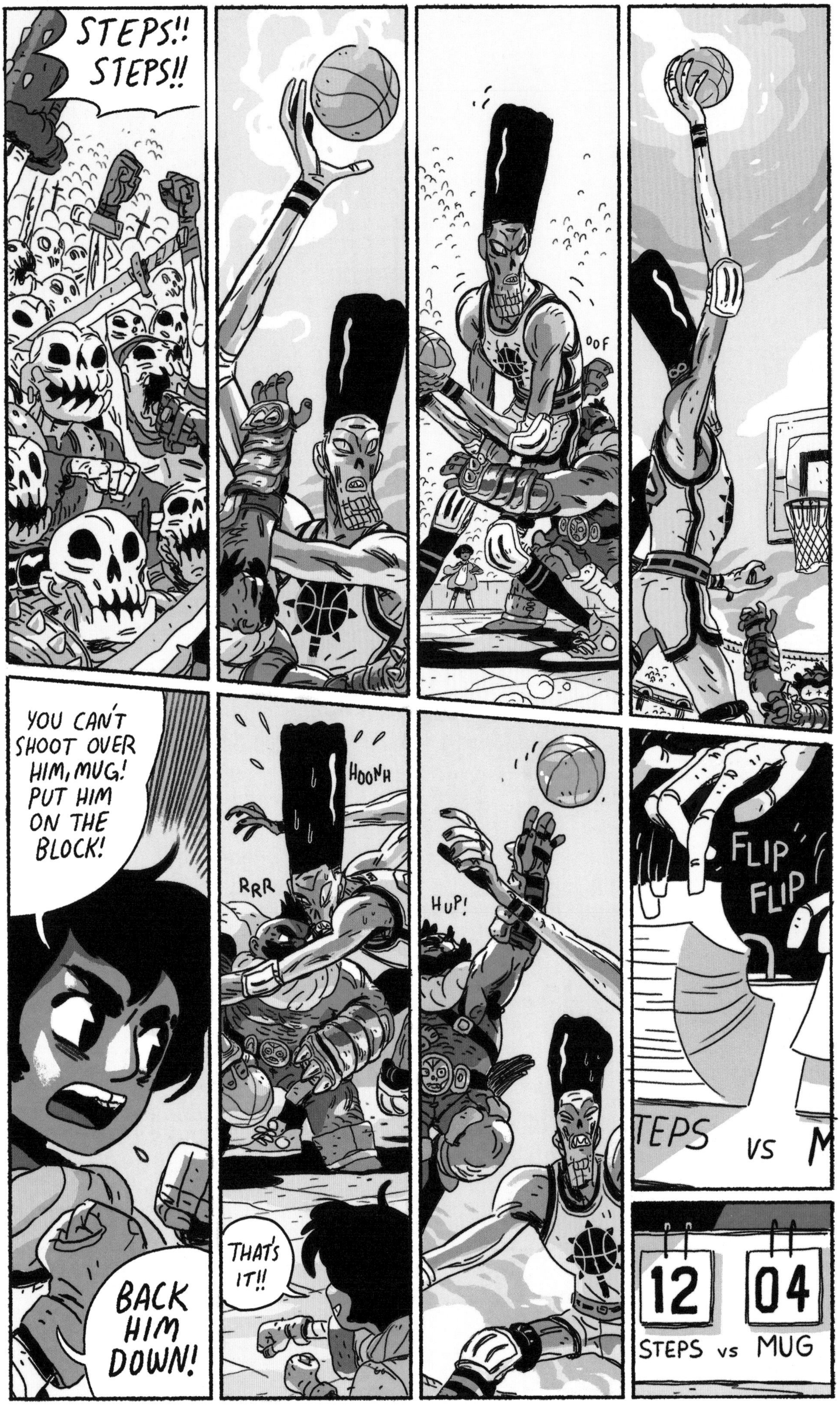
STEPS!! STEPS!!
OOF
YOU CAN'T SHOOT OVER HIM, MUG! PUT HIM ON THE BLOCK!
BACK HIM DOWN!
HOONH
RRR
THAT'S IT!!
HUP!
FLIP
FLIP
TEPS VS M
12
04
STEPS vs MUG

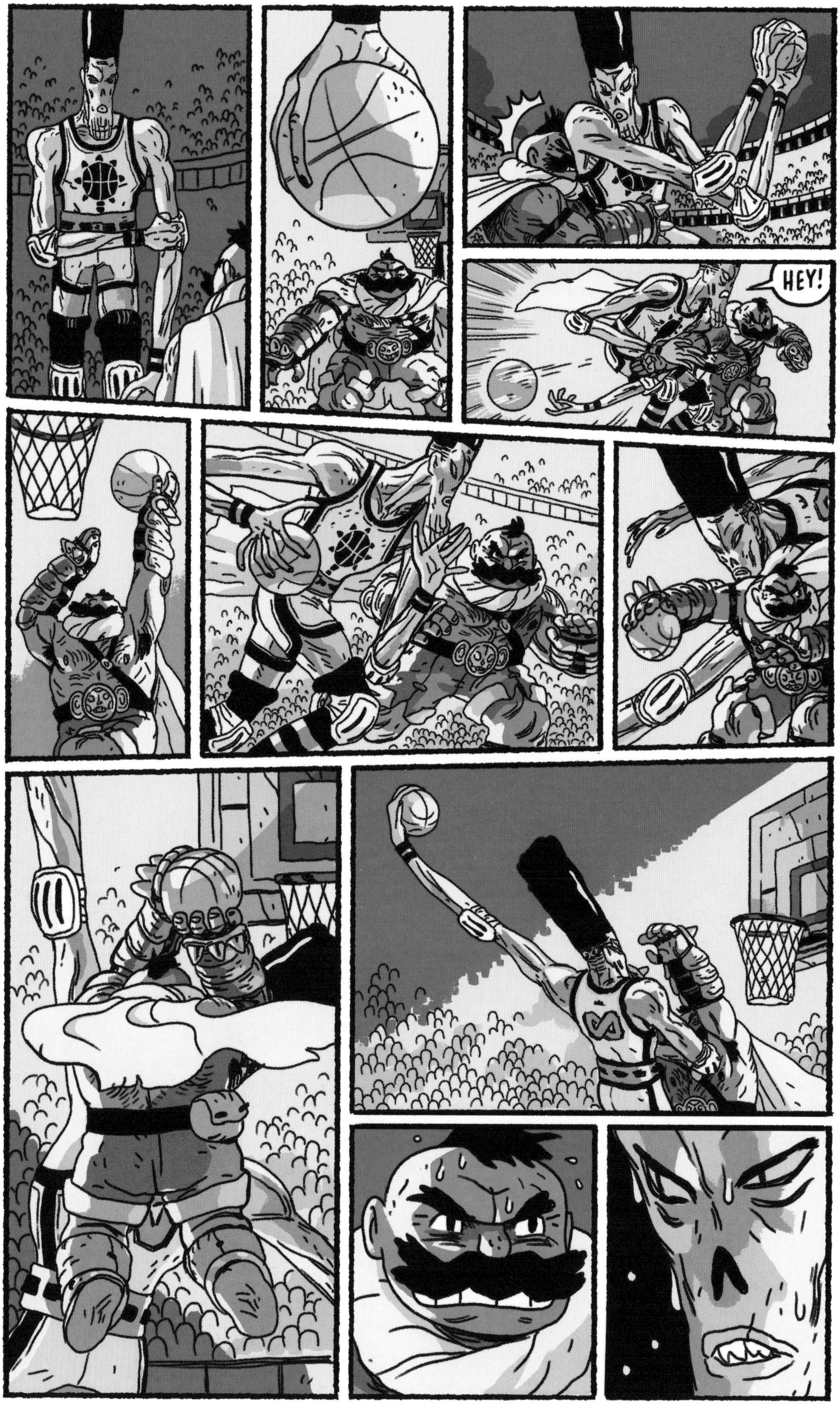
HEY!

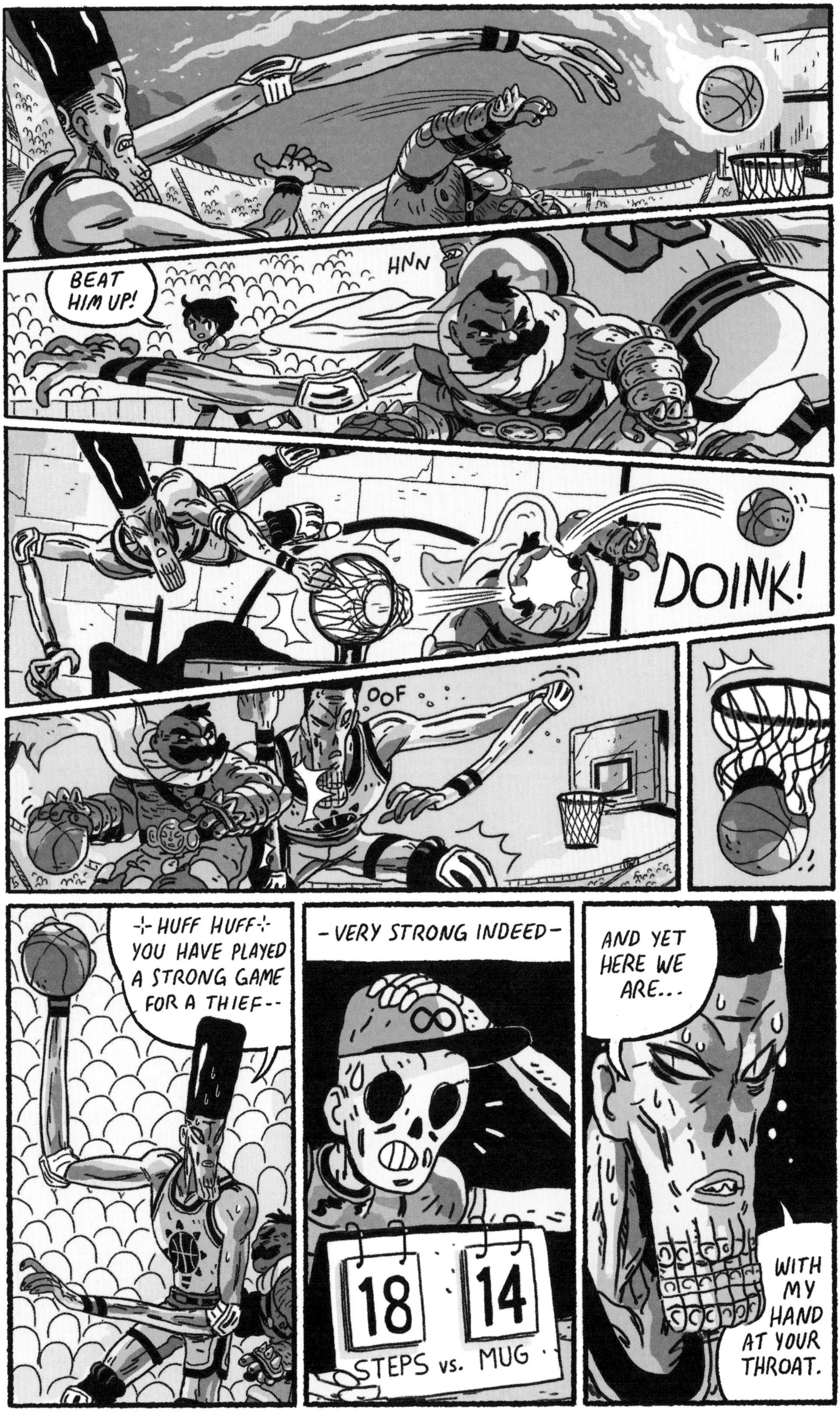
BEAT HIM UP!
HNN
DOINK!
OOF
-¦- HUFF HUFF -¦- YOU HAVE PLAYED A STRONG GAME FOR A THIEF--
- VERY STRONG INDEED -
18
14
STEPS vs. MUG
AND YET HERE WE ARE...
WITH MY HAND AT YOUR THROAT.

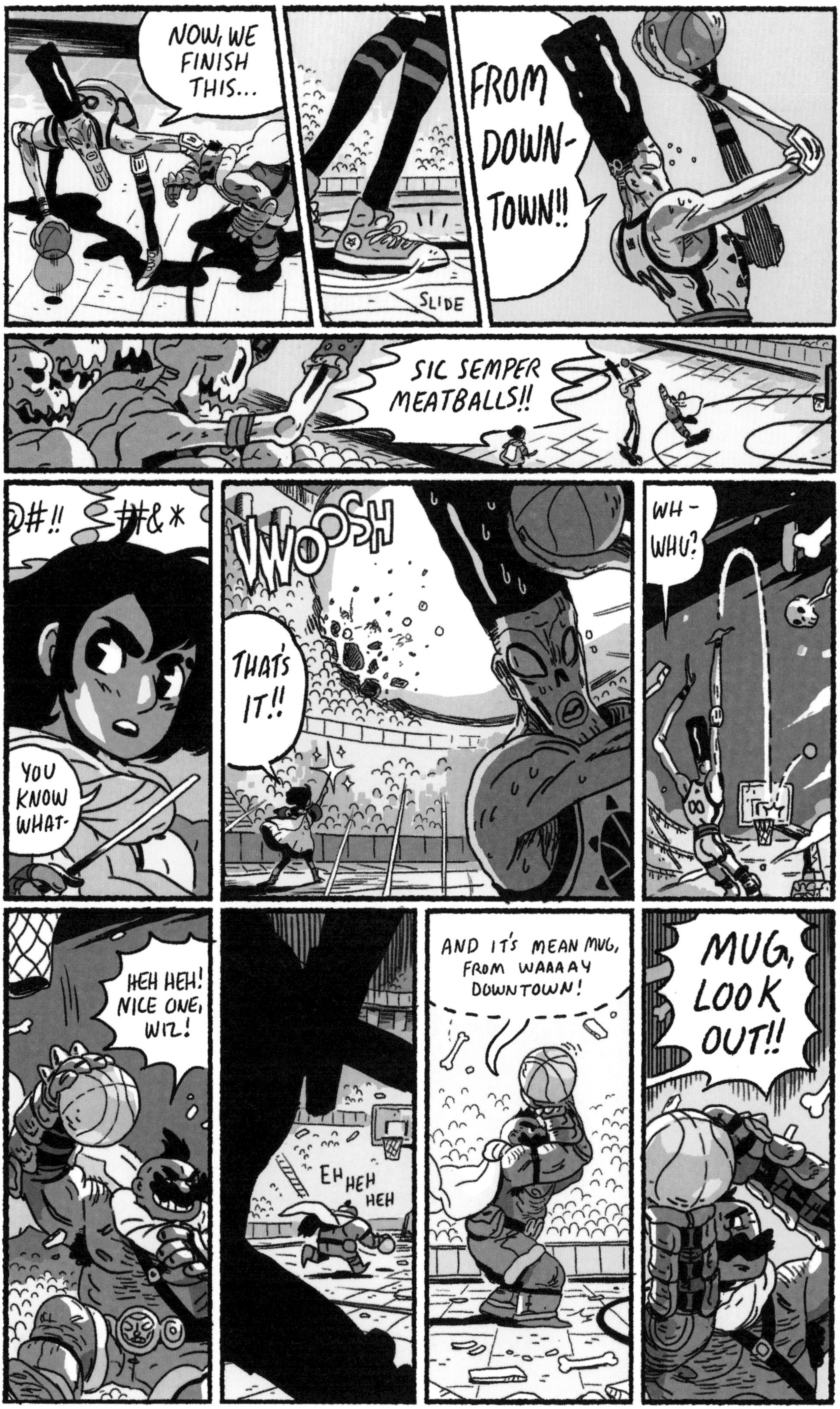
NOW, WE FINISH THIS...
SLIDE
FROM DOWN-TOWN!!
SIC SEMPER MEATBALLS!!
@#!! ##&*
YOU KNOW WHAT-
VWOOSH
THAT'S IT!!
WH-WHU?
HEH HEH! NICE ONE, WIZ!
EH HEH HEH
AND IT'S MEAN MUG, FROM WAAAAY DOWNTOWN!
MUG, LOOK OUT!!

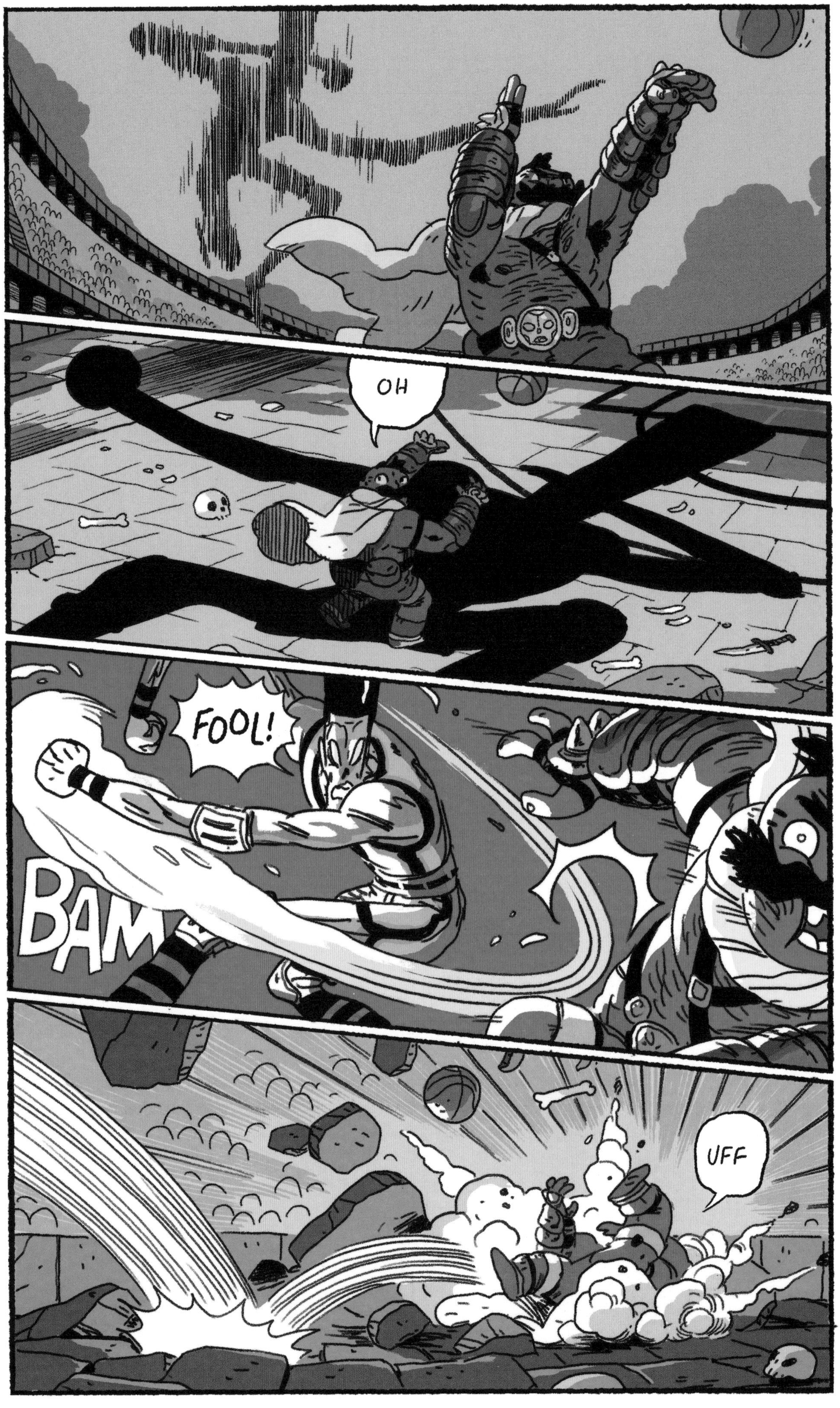
OH
FOOL!
BAM
UFF

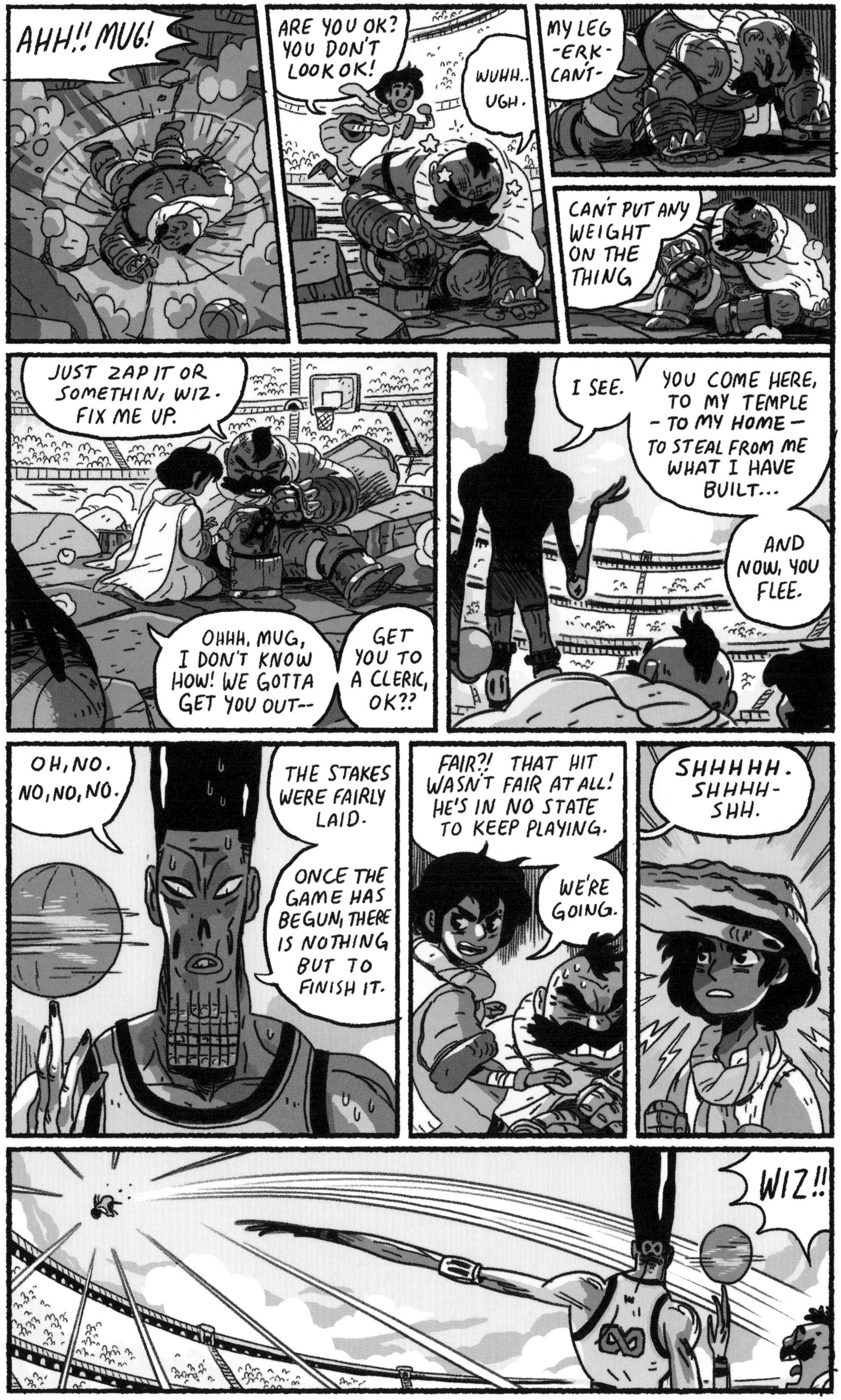
AHH!! MUG!
ARE YOU OK? YOU DON'T LOOK OK!
WUHH.. UGH.
MY LEG -ERK- CAN'T-
CAN'T PUT ANY WEIGHT ON THE THING
JUST ZAP IT OR SOMETHIN, WIZ. FIX ME UP.
OHHH, MUG, I DON'T KNOW HOW! WE GOTTA GET YOU OUT--
GET YOU TO A CLERIC, OK??
I SEE.
YOU COME HERE, TO MY TEMPLE - TO MY HOME - TO STEAL FROM ME WHAT I HAVE BUILT...
AND NOW, YOU FLEE.
OH, NO. NO, NO, NO.
THE STAKES WERE FAIRLY LAID.
ONCE THE GAME HAS BEGUN, THERE IS NOTHING BUT TO FINISH IT.
FAIR?! THAT HIT WASN'T FAIR AT ALL! HE'S IN NO STATE TO KEEP PLAYING.
WE'RE GOING.
SHHHHH. SHHHH-SHH.
WIZ!!

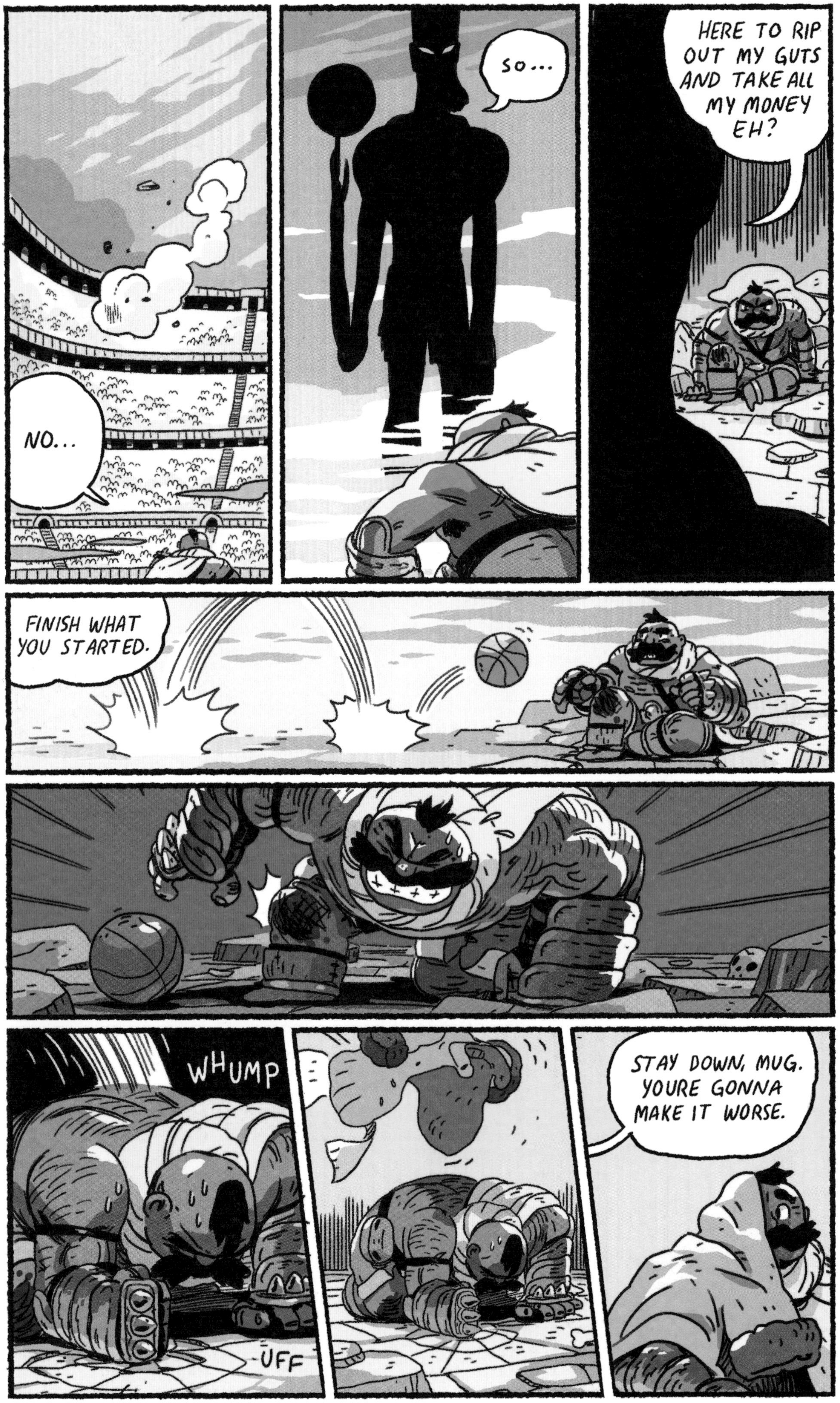
NO...
SO...
HERE TO RIP OUT MY GUTS AND TAKE ALL MY MONEY EH?
FINISH WHAT YOU STARTED.
WHUMP
UFF
STAY DOWN, MUG. YOURE GONNA MAKE IT WORSE.

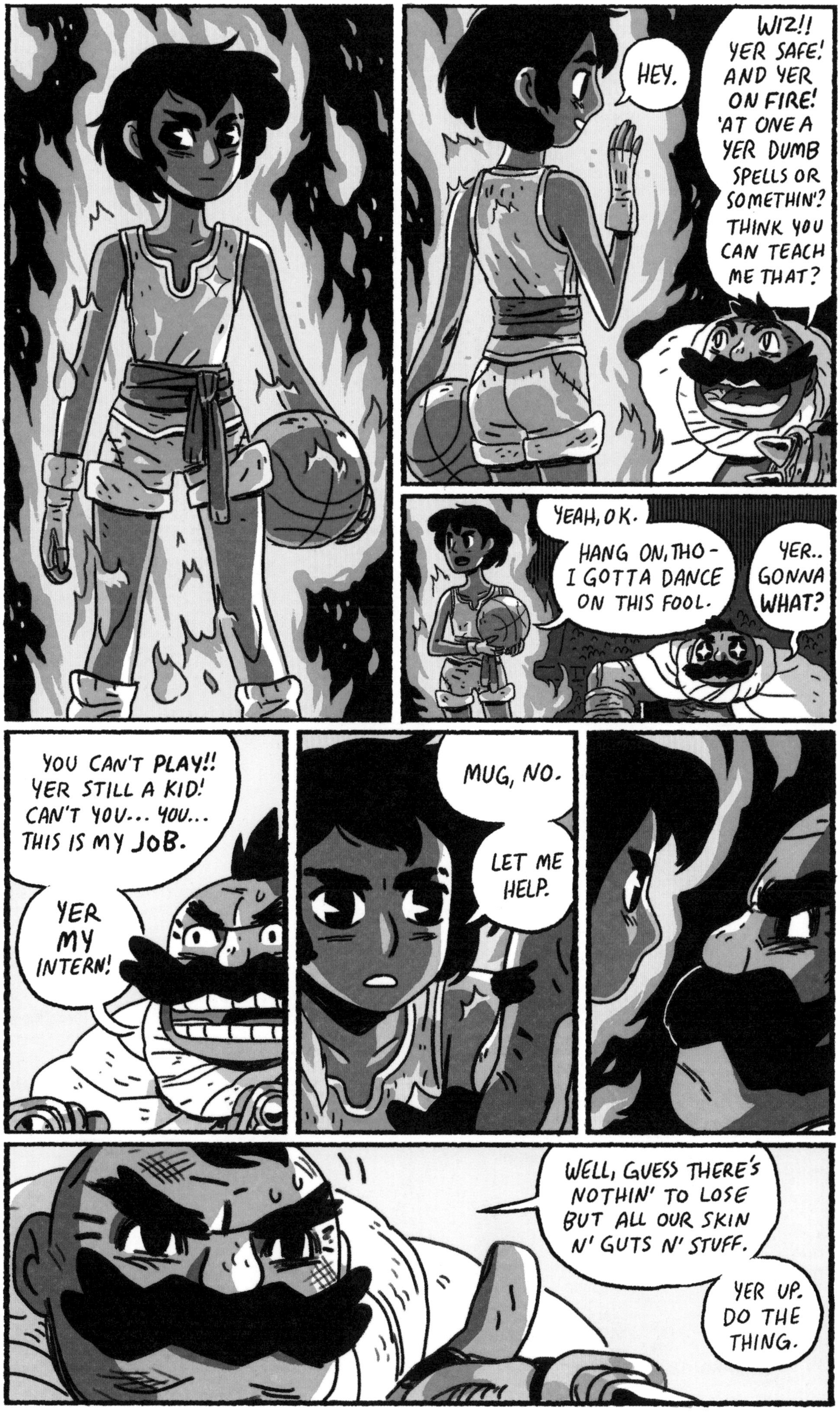
HEY.
WIZ!! YER SAFE! AND YER ON FIRE! 'AT ONE A YER DUMB SPELLS OR SOMETHIN'? THINK YOU CAN TEACH ME THAT?
YEAH, OK.
HANG ON, THO - I GOTTA DANCE ON THIS FOOL.
YER.. GONNA WHAT?
YOU CAN'T PLAY!! YER STILL A KID! CAN'T YOU... YOU... THIS IS MY JOB.
YER MY INTERN!
MUG, NO.
LET ME HELP.
WELL, GUESS THERE'S NOTHIN' TO LOSE BUT ALL OUR SKIN N' GUTS N' STUFF.
YER UP. DO THE THING.

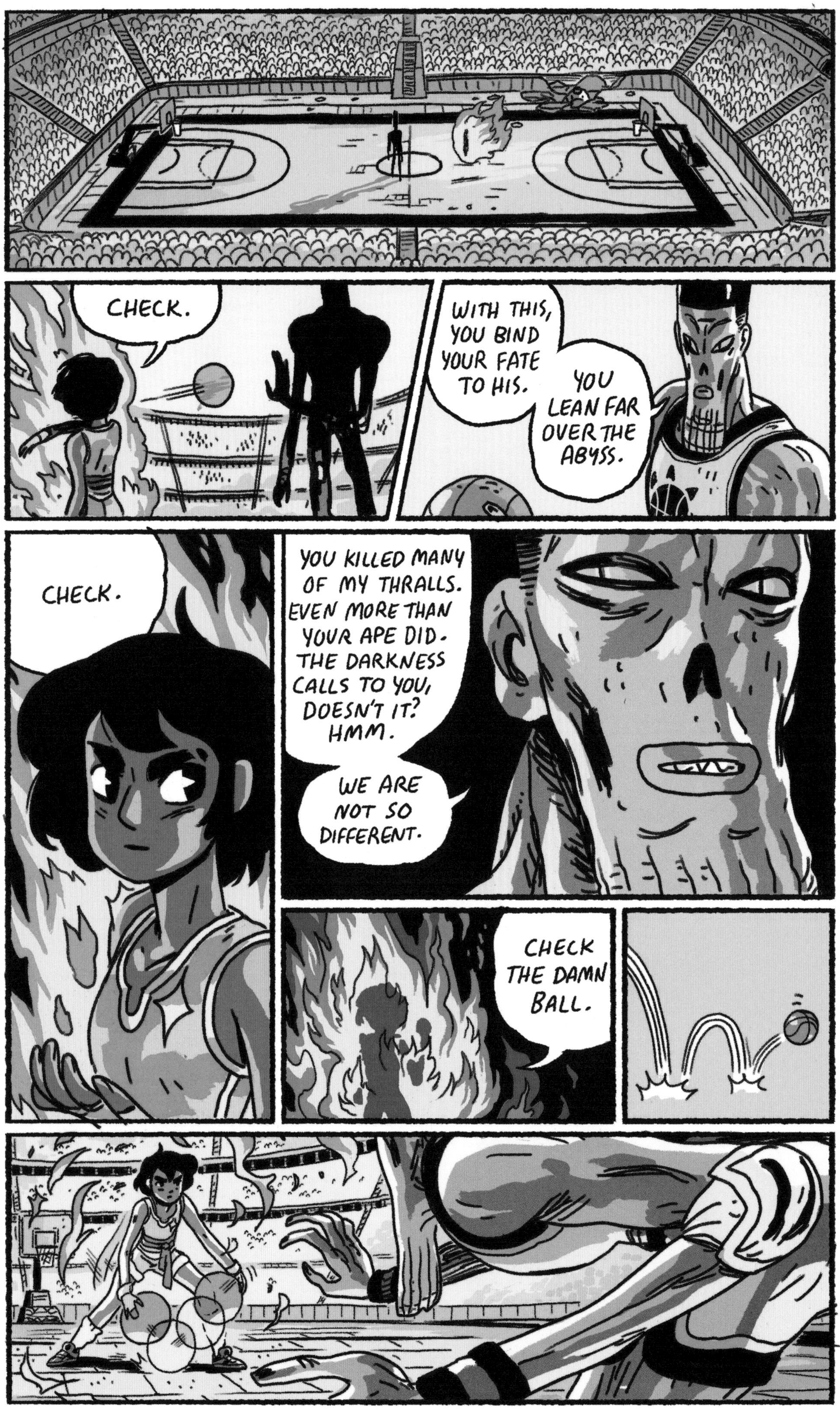
CHECK.
WITH THIS, YOU BIND YOUR FATE TO HIS.
YOU LEAN FAR OVER THE ABYSS.
CHECK.
YOU KILLED MANY OF MY THRALLS. EVEN MORE THAN YOUR APE DID. THE DARKNESS CALLS TO YOU, DOESN'T IT? HMM.
WE ARE NOT SO DIFFERENT.
CHECK THE DAMN BALL.

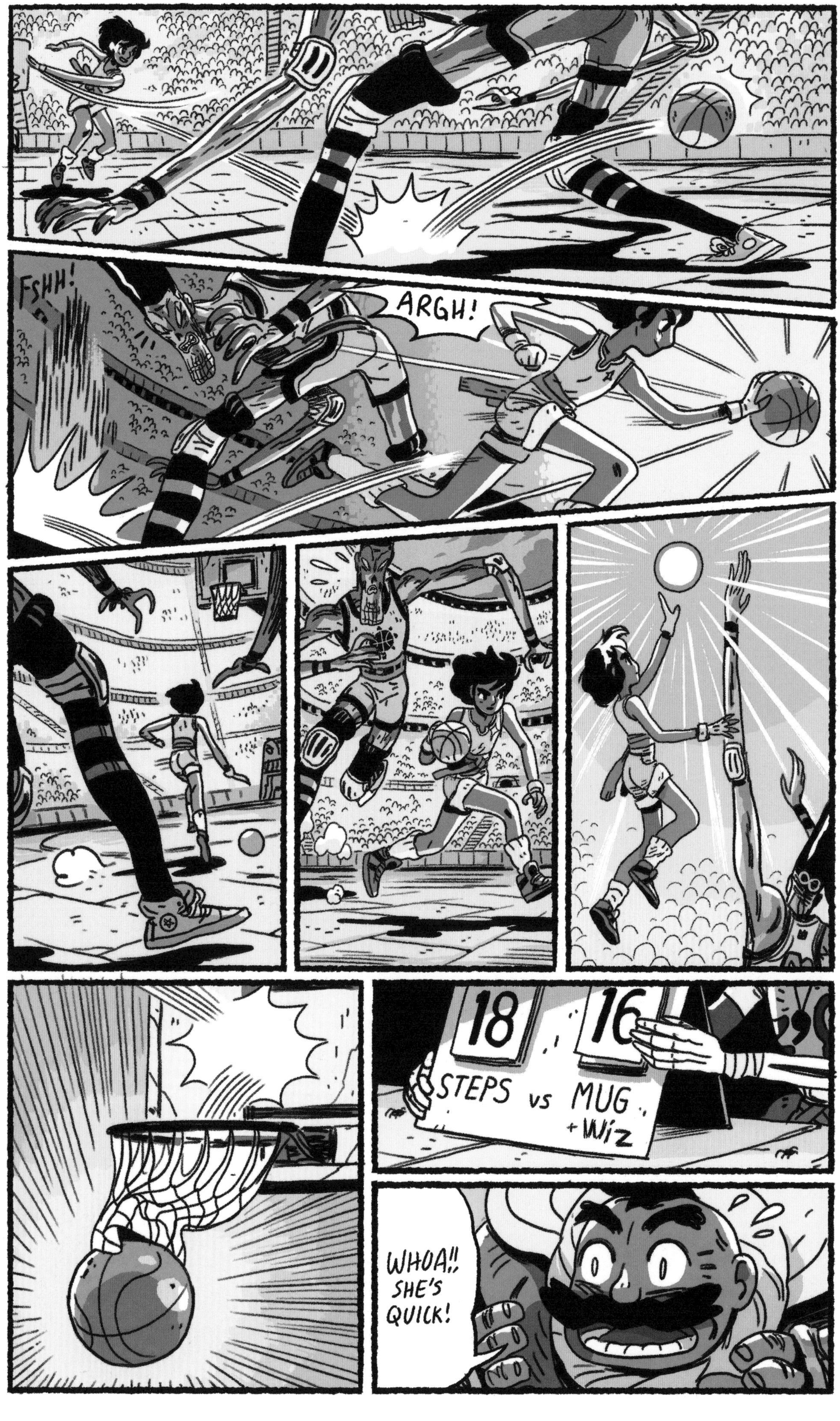
FSHH!
ARGH!
18
16
STEPS vs MUG
+ Wiz
WHOA!! SHE'S QUICK!

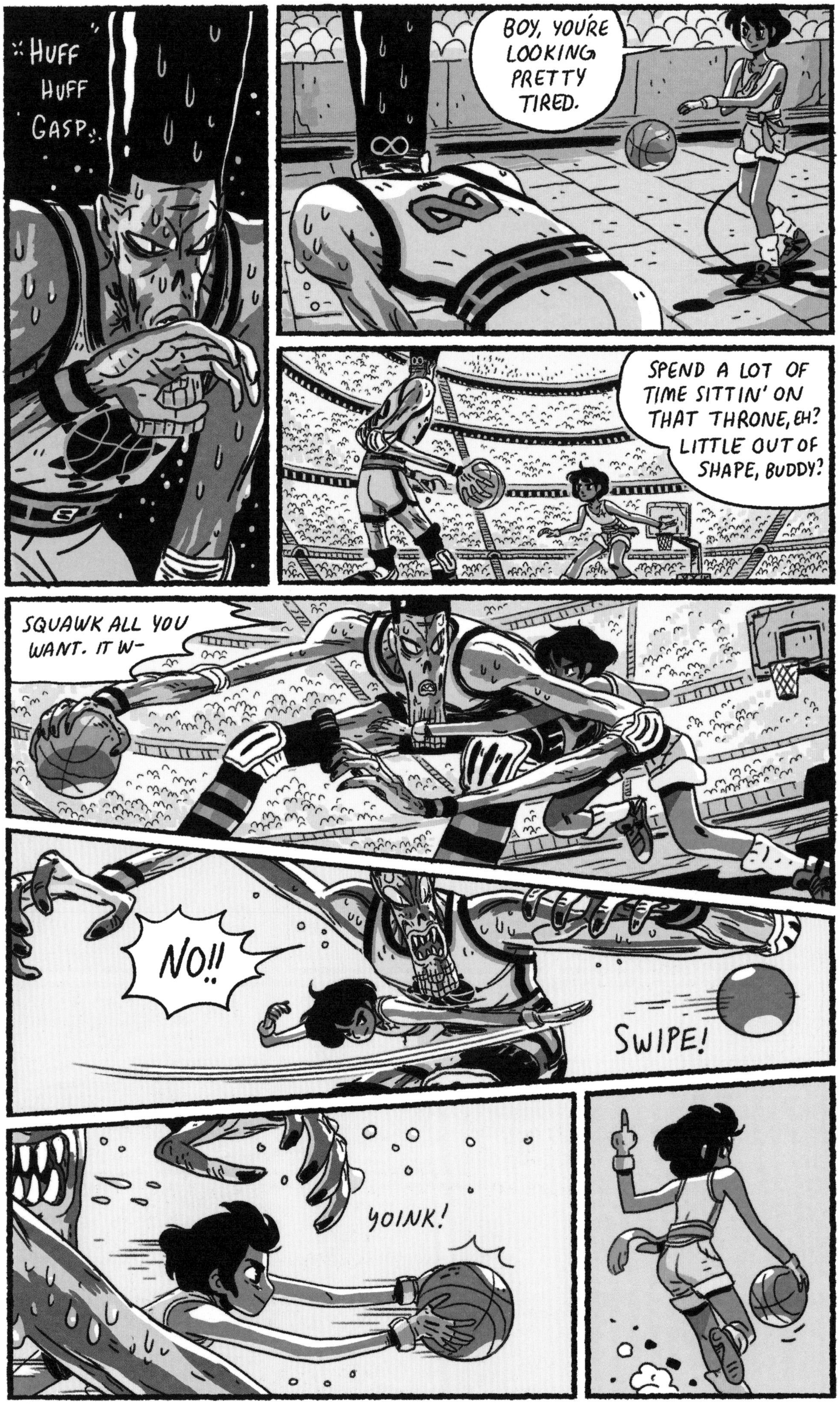
HUFF
HUFF
GASP
BOY, YOU'RE LOOKING PRETTY TIRED.
SPEND A LOT OF TIME SITTIN' ON THAT THRONE, EH? LITTLE OUT OF SHAPE, BUDDY?
SQUAWK ALL YOU WANT. IT W-
NO!!
SWIPE!
YOINK!

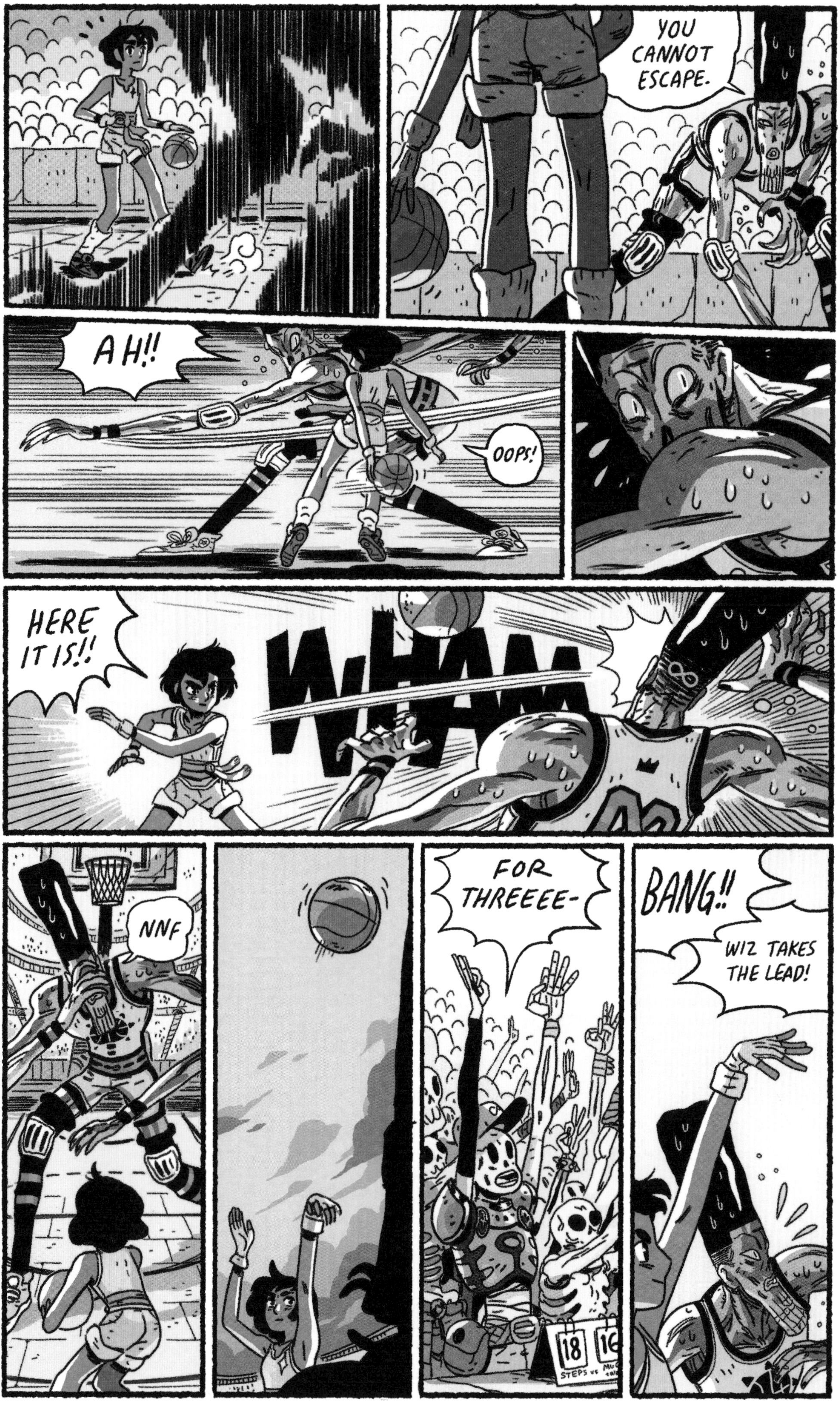
YOU CANNOT ESCAPE.
AH!!
OOPS!
HERE IT IS!!
WHAM
NNF
FOR THREEEE-
18
16
STEPS VS
BANG!!
WIZ TAKES THE LEAD!

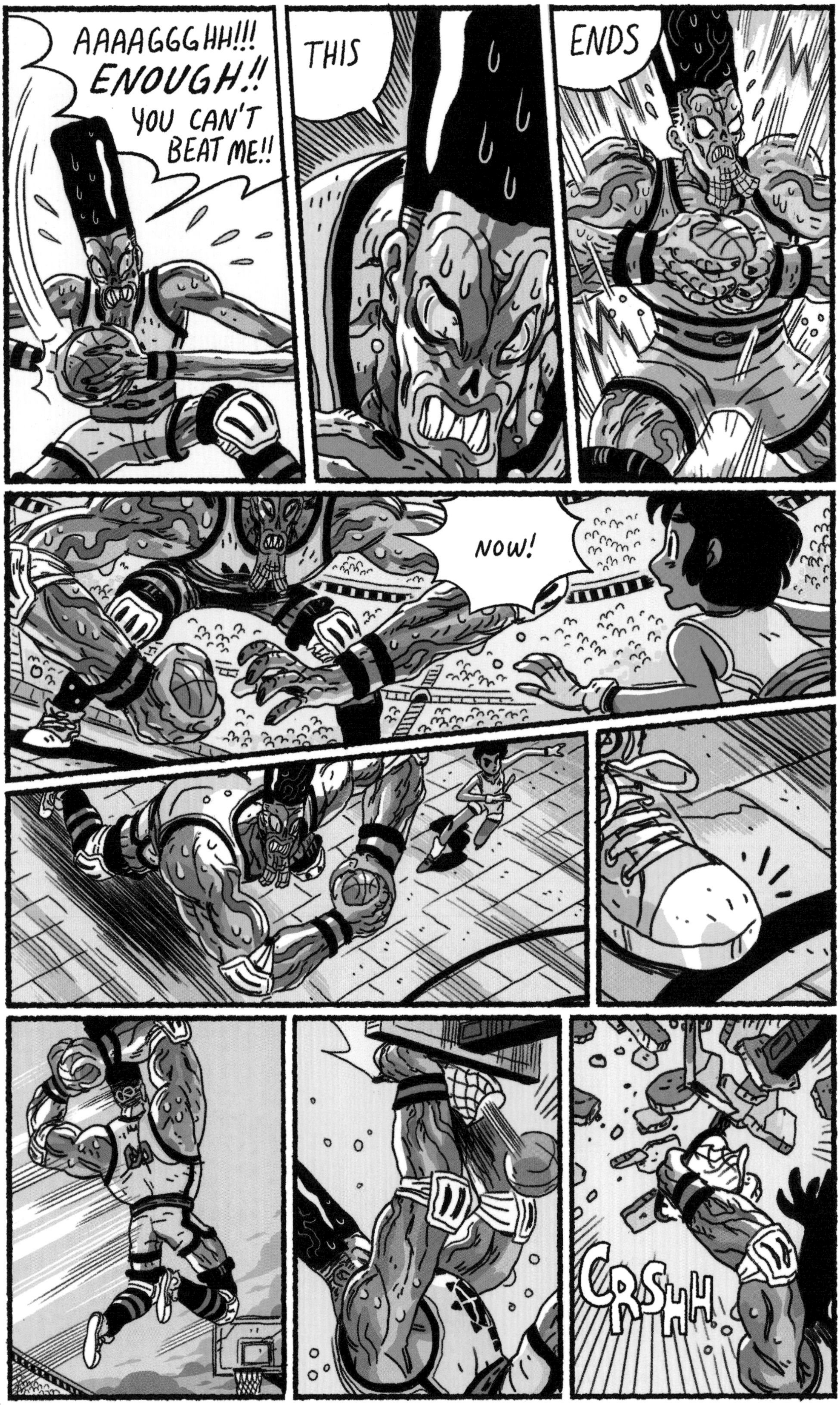
AAAAGGGHH!!! ENOUGH!! YOU CAN'T BEAT ME!!
THIS
ENDS
NOW!
CRSHH

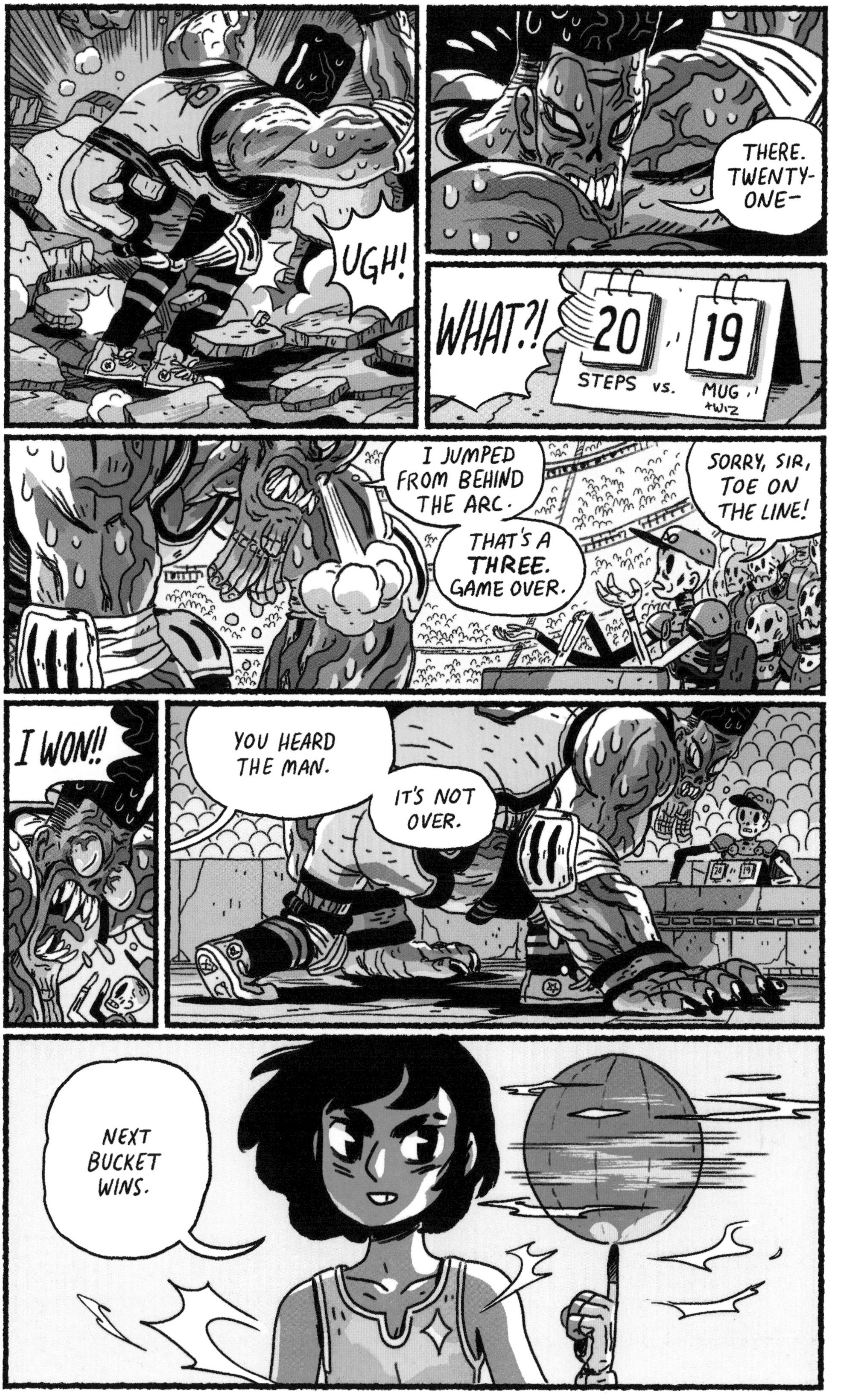
UGH!
THERE. TWENTY-ONE–
WHAT?!
20 19
STEPS vs. MUG +WIZ
I JUMPED FROM BEHIND THE ARC.
THAT'S A THREE. GAME OVER.
SORRY, SIR, TOE ON THE LINE!
I WON!!
YOU HEARD THE MAN.
IT'S NOT OVER.
NEXT BUCKET WINS.

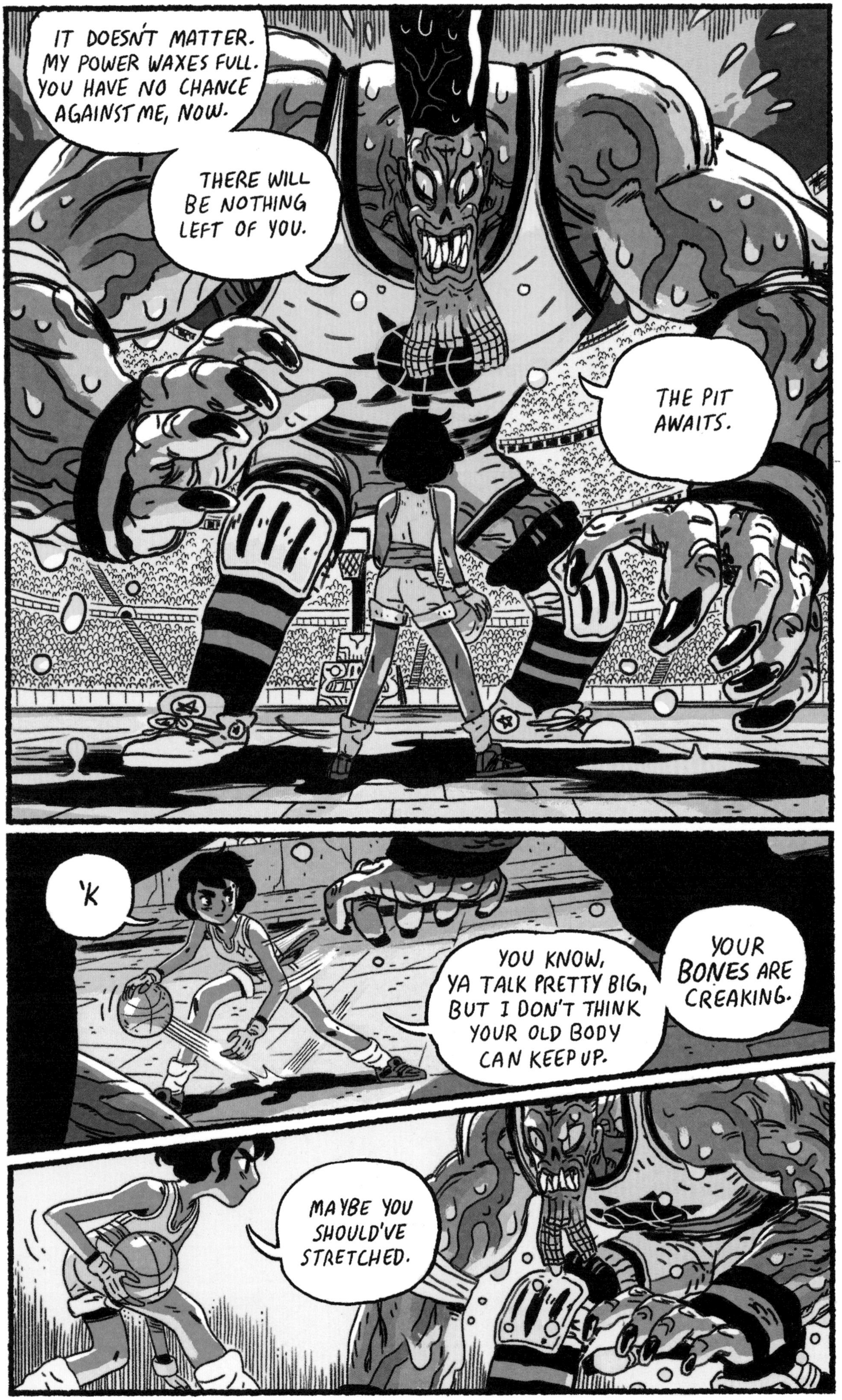
IT DOESN'T MATTER. MY POWER WAXES FULL. YOU HAVE NO CHANCE AGAINST ME, NOW.
THERE WILL BE NOTHING LEFT OF YOU.
THE PIT AWAITS.
'K
YOU KNOW, YA TALK PRETTY BIG, BUT I DON'T THINK YOUR OLD BODY CAN KEEP UP.
YOUR BONES ARE CREAKING.
MAYBE YOU SHOULD'VE STRETCHED.

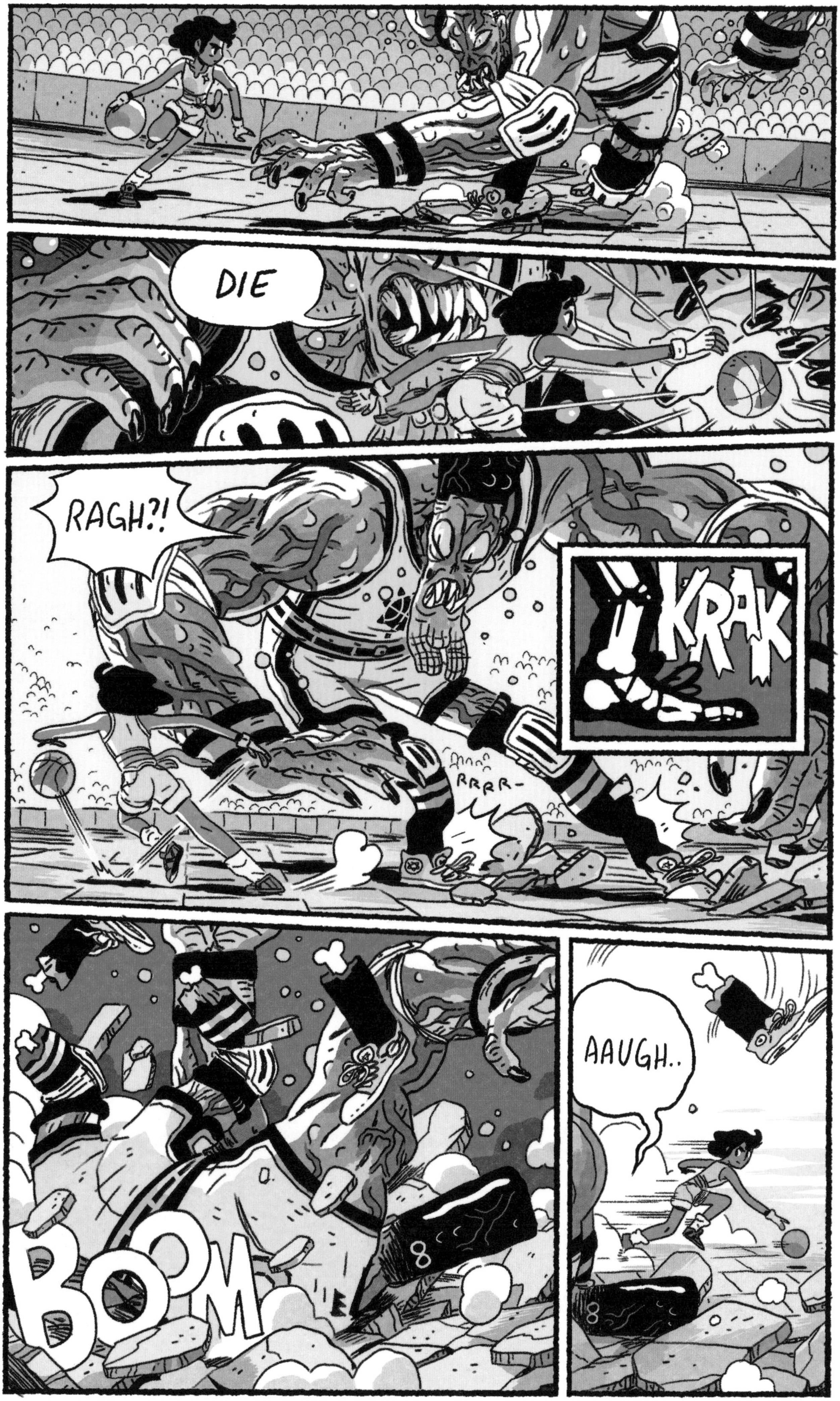
DIE
RAGH?!
KRAK
RRRR-
BOOM
AAUGH..

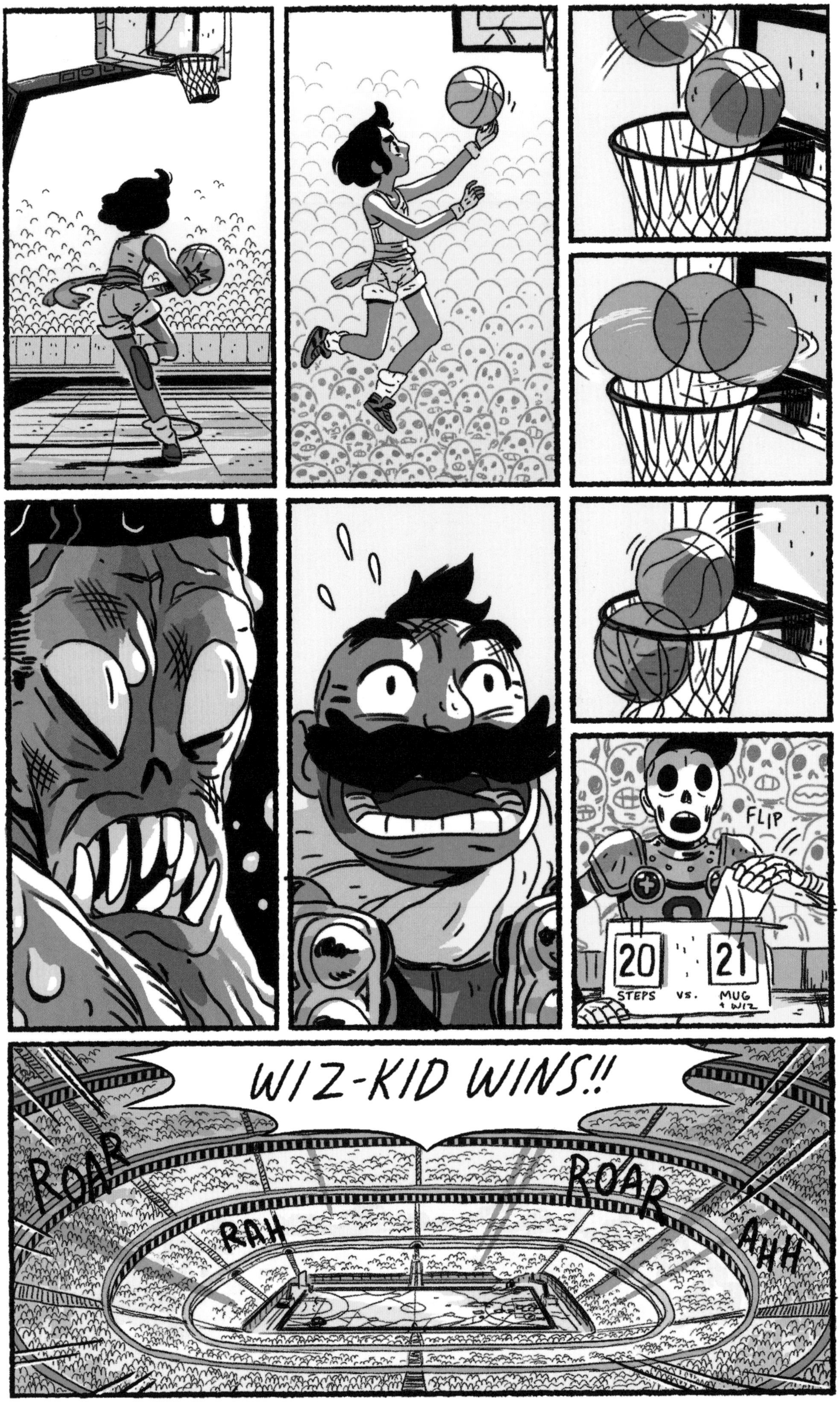
FLIP
20
21
STEPS VS. MUG + WIZ
WIZ-KID WINS!!
ROAR
RAH
ROAR
AHH

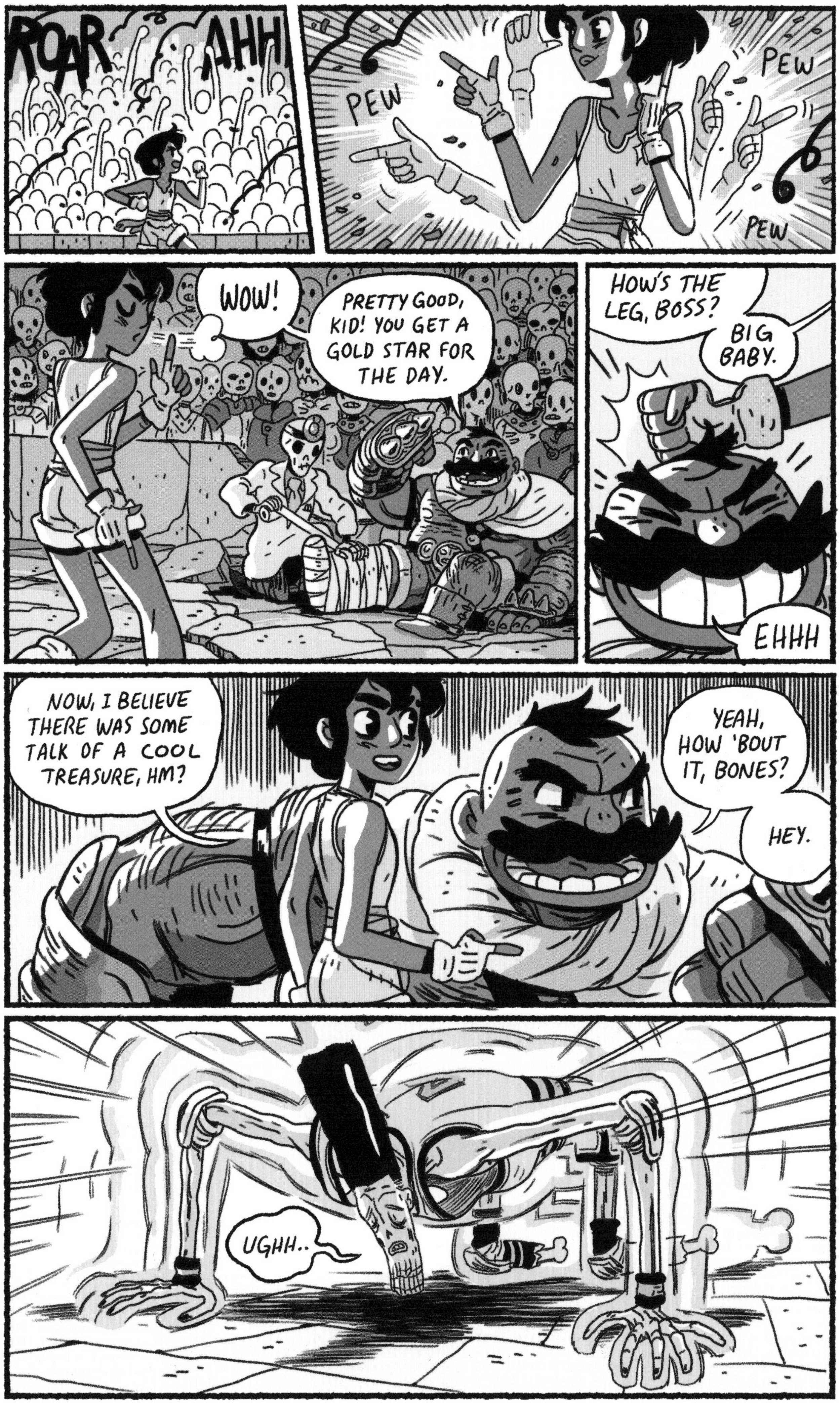
ROAR
AHH
PEW
PEW
PEW
WOW!
PRETTY GOOD, KID! YOU GET A GOLD STAR FOR THE DAY.
HOW'S THE LEG, BOSS?
BIG BABY.
EHHH
NOW, I BELIEVE THERE WAS SOME TALK OF A COOL TREASURE, HM?
YEAH, HOW 'BOUT IT, BONES?
HEY.
UGHH..

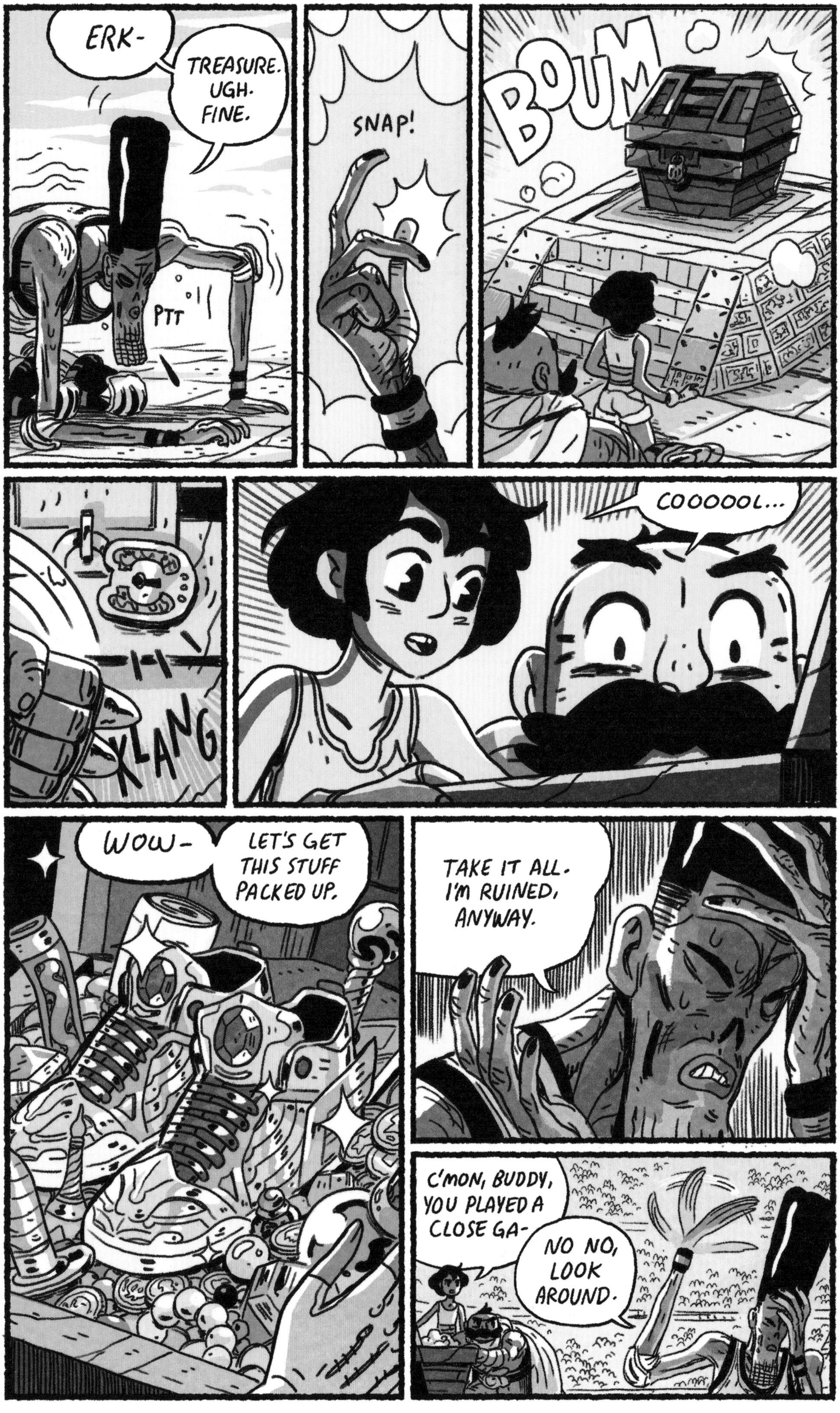
ERK-
TREASURE. UGH. FINE.
PTT
SNAP!
BOUM
KLANG
COOOOOL...
WOW-
LET'S GET THIS STUFF PACKED UP.
TAKE IT ALL. I'M RUINED, ANYWAY.
C'MON, BUDDY, YOU PLAYED A CLOSE GA-
NO NO, LOOK AROUND.

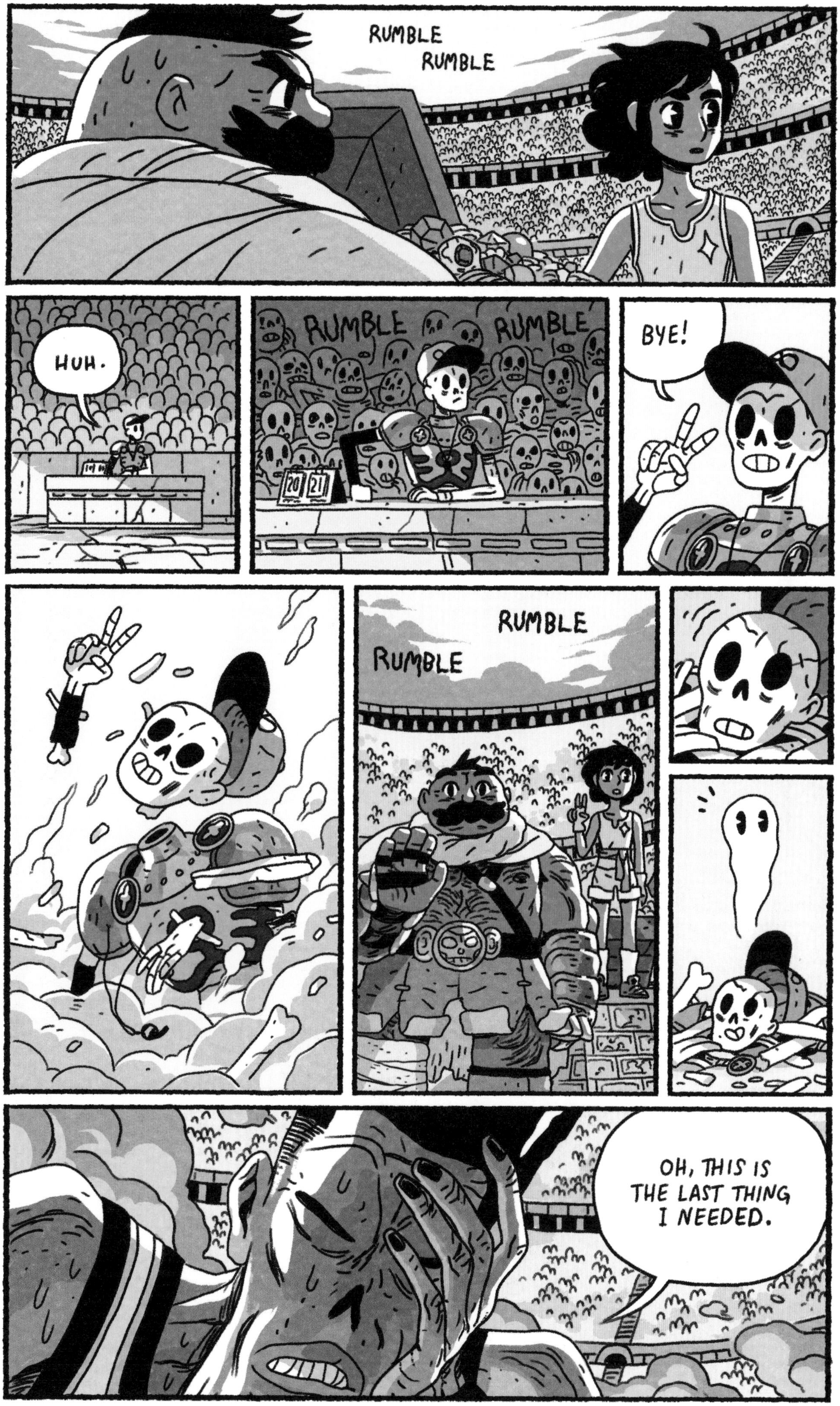
RUMBLE
RUMBLE
HUH.
RUMBLE RUMBLE
BYE!
RUMBLE
RUMBLE
OH, THIS IS THE LAST THING I NEEDED.

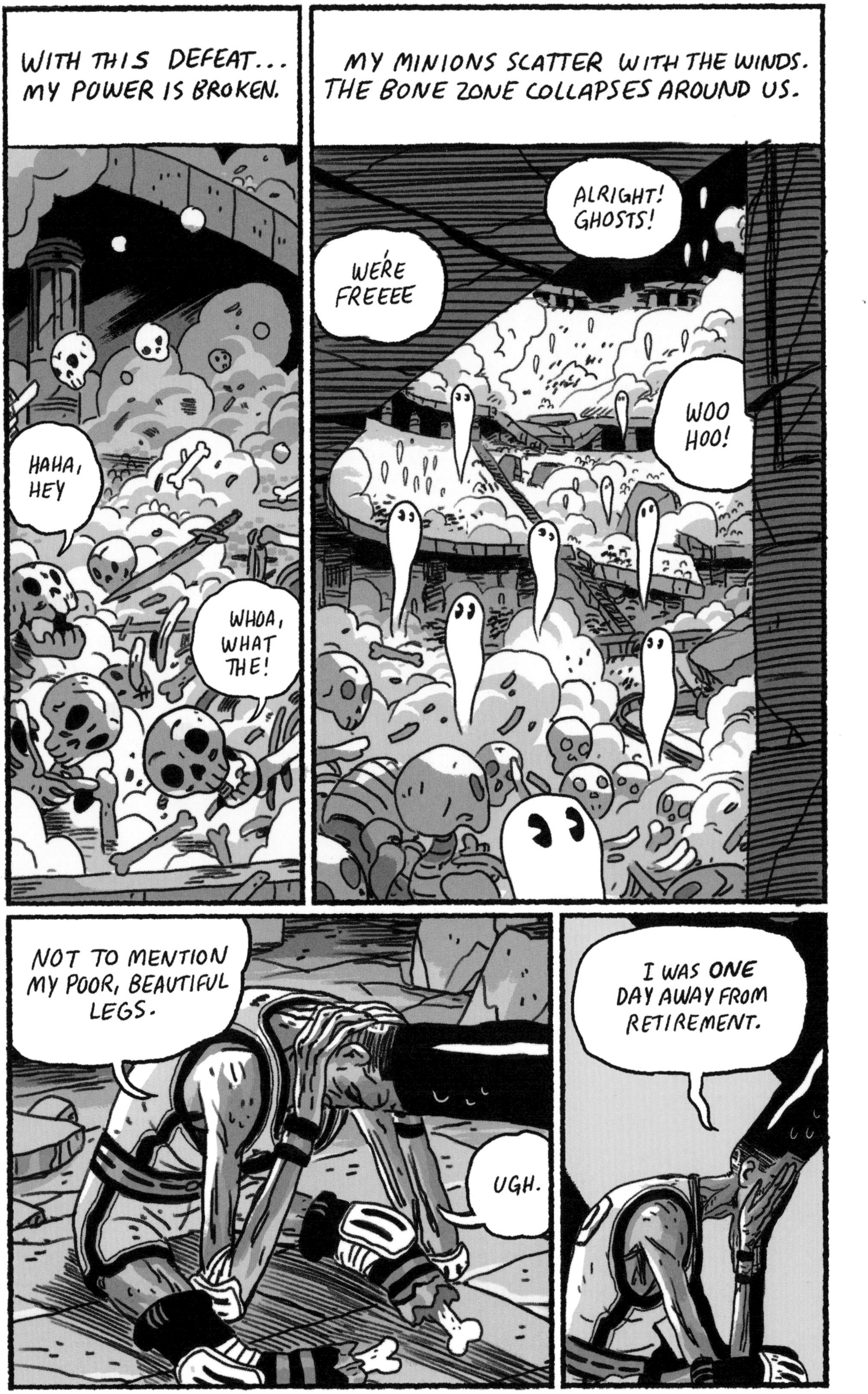
WITH THIS DEFEAT... MY POWER IS BROKEN.
HAHA, HEY
WHOA, WHAT THE!
MY MINIONS SCATTER WITH THE WINDS. THE BONE ZONE COLLAPSES AROUND US.
WE'RE FREEEE
ALRIGHT! GHOSTS!
WOO HOO!
NOT TO MENTION MY POOR, BEAUTIFUL LEGS.
UGH.
I WAS ONE DAY AWAY FROM RETIREMENT.

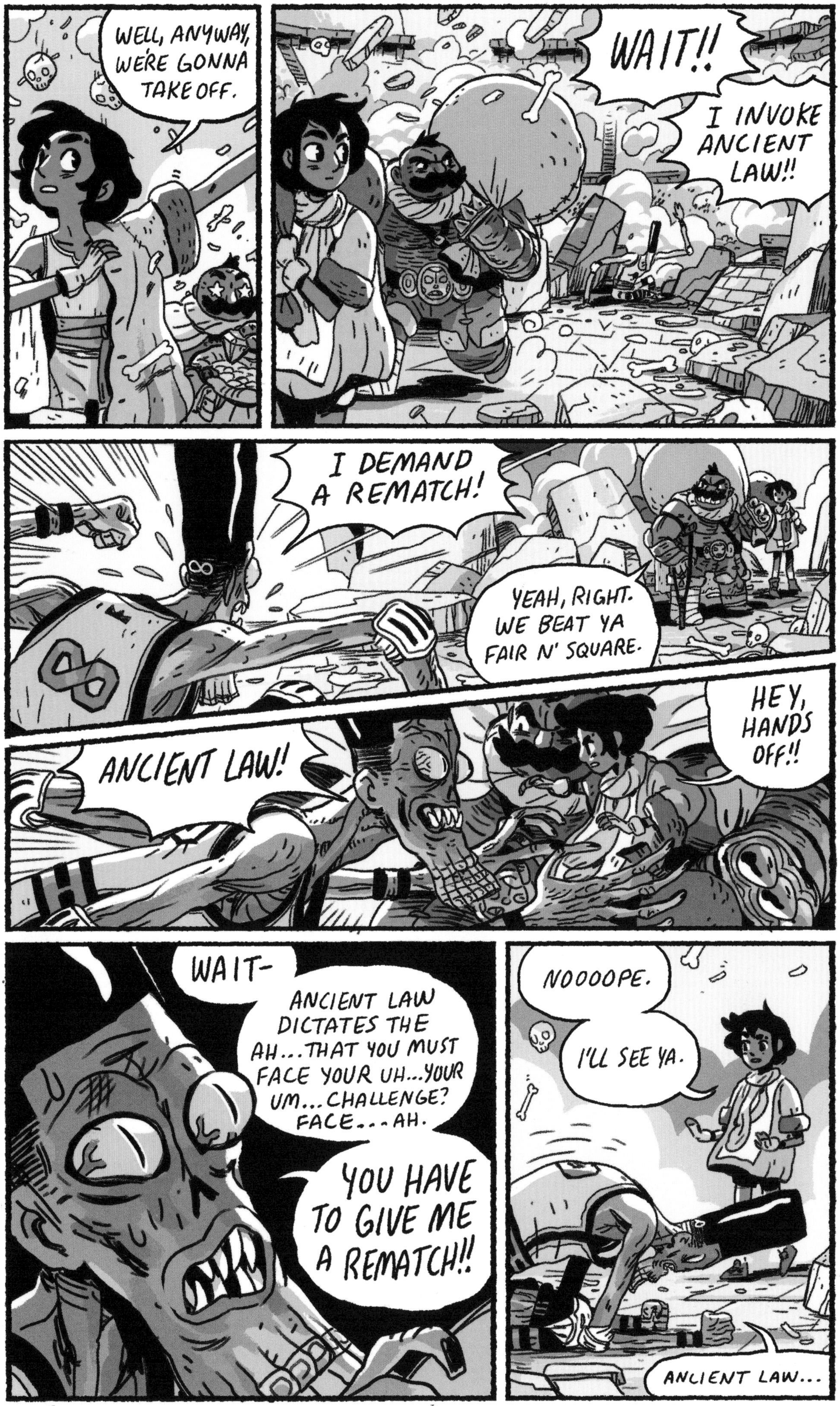
WELL, ANYWAY, WE'RE GONNA TAKE OFF.
WAIT!!
I INVOKE ANCIENT LAW!!
I DEMAND A REMATCH!
YEAH, RIGHT. WE BEAT YA FAIR N' SQUARE.
ANCIENT LAW!
HEY, HANDS OFF!!
WAIT-
ANCIENT LAW DICTATES THE AH... THAT YOU MUST FACE YOUR UH... YOUR UM... CHALLENGE? FACE... AH.
YOU HAVE TO GIVE ME A REMATCH!!
NOOOOPE.
I'LL SEE YA.
ANCIENT LAW...

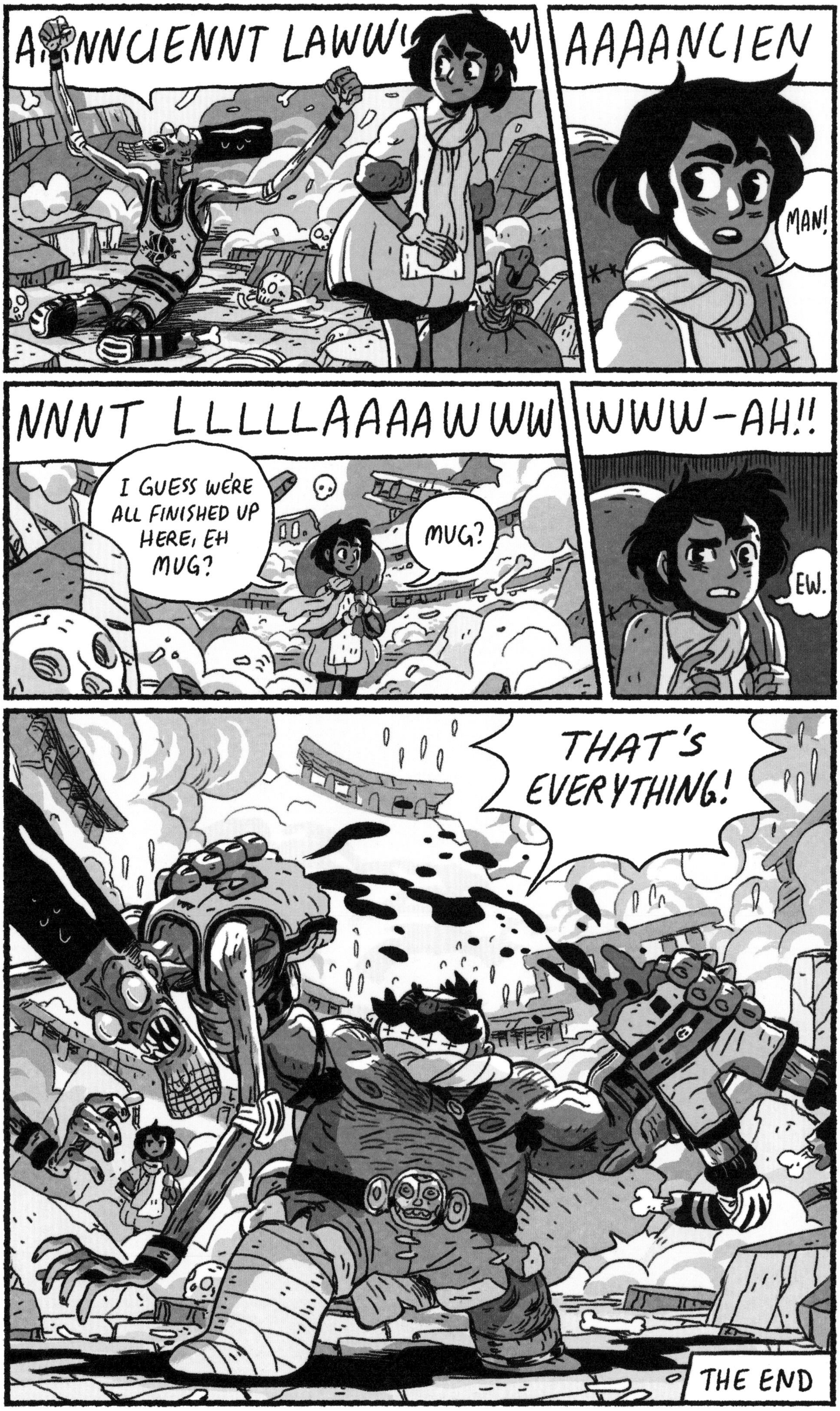

AANNCIENNT LAWW!
AAAANCIEN
MAN!
NNNT LLLLLAAAAWWW
I GUESS WE'RE ALL FINISHED UP HERE, EH MUG?
MUG?
WWW-AH!!
EW.
THAT'S EVERYTHING!
THE END

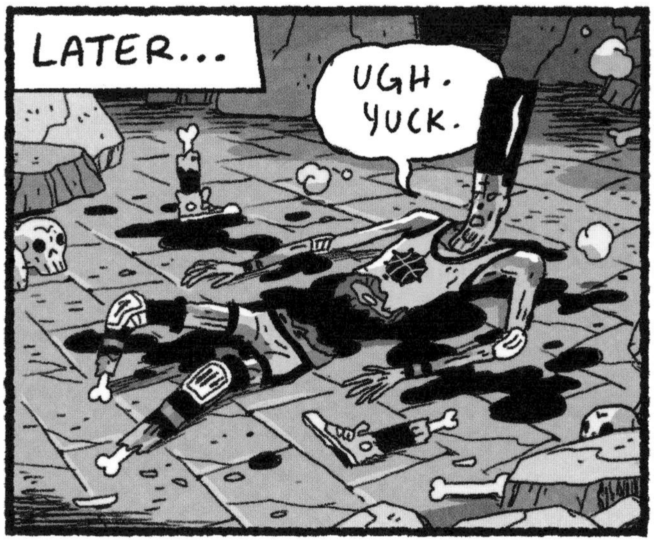
LATER...
UGH. YUCK.

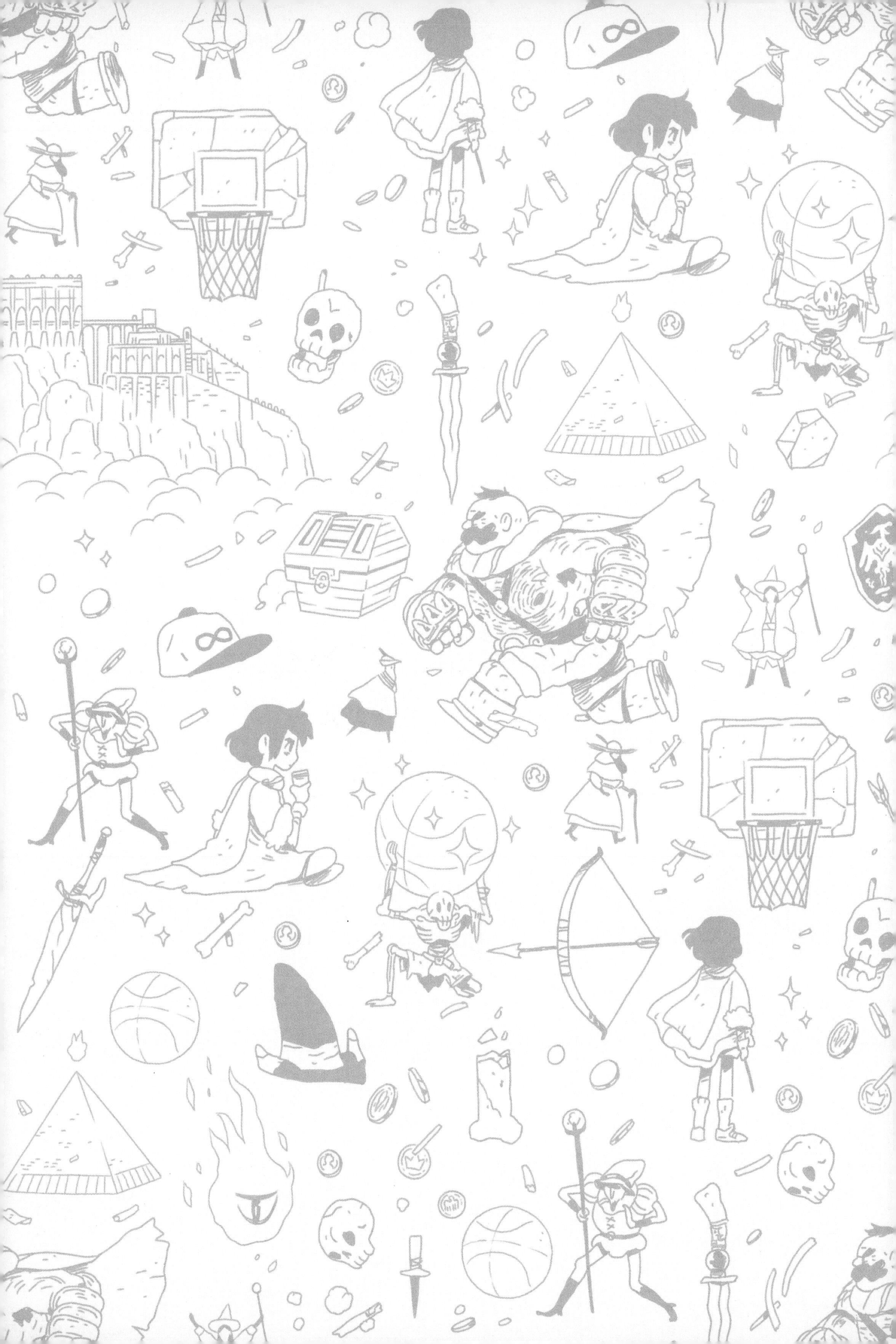